To our good friends,
Peter and Hilary O'Farrelly,
who assisted us not only with their
encouragement, knowledge and suggestions
but also by reading the manuscript.
Go méadaí Dia a stór.

WILD AND FREE

Cooking from Nature

Wild food is growing in abundance all around us on hedgerows and hillsides free for the taking. Throughout most of the world wild food foraging is a way of life that has been handed down from generation to generation, but in our modern way of life the wild food knowledge and skills that our not-so-distant ancestors cherished, have all but disappeared.
Wild and Free was first published in 1978 by husband and wife team, Cyril and Kit Ó Céirín. Through their love of folklore and tradition they collected many recipes and skills handed down from previous generations. Cyril (1934-1999) was an author, painter, translator, environmentalist, and award-winning poet of national prominence. Fellow author, Kit inherited many traditional recipes and has used wild foods for years in her cooking. She is a passionate environmentalist and continues to write and publish on a variety of subjects. Books published by the Ó Céiríns include *The Women of Ireland: A Biographic Dictionary, The Outlandish World of the Burren, The Road to Lisdoonvarna,* translations of *Séadna* and *Mo Scéal Féin.*

This is an empowering book, a book that illustrates, interprets, groups and documents and it does all this, for the lay person, the cook or gardener who wants information and nourishment from what lies abundantly around us. The Ó Céiríns' sense of enquiry demystifies these foods, whilst at the same time adding to their mythology.
Sally McKenna

Wild and Free is a book that should be in every house.
Irish Times

It's the mixture of practical information, commonsense and literary and mythological allusions that makes this book so attractive.
Irish Farmer's Journal

The book is intended for a wide readership not just dedicated nature lovers.
Irish Independent

WILD AND FREE

cooking from nature

New Introduction by Sally McKenna

BY CYRIL & KIT Ó CÉIRÍN

Illustrations by Cyril Ó Céirín

Wolf Hill Publishing

First published 1978 by
The O'Brien Press Ltd., Dublin.

This edition published 2013 by
Wolf Hill Publishing/Cló Cnocán an Mhic Tíre,
Teach Radharc an Atlantaigh, Lios Dúin Bhearna, Co. an Chláir.

A catalogue record for this title is available from the British Library.
ISBN: 978 0 9554907-4-3

Layout and Design by Vincent Casey

Printed and bound in Ireland
By Hudson Killeen Ltd.

CONTENTS

CODE OF PRACTICE

For the responsible harvesting of food from the wild

Foraging for wild food should not be seen as an unrestricted natural larder and we should behave responsibly while at the same time enjoying the wonderful bounty that nature has given us.

...Do not strip the food resource bare - only harvest a small amount from each source. Allow enough seed for the plant to regenerate - removing all the flowers, seeds, berries will largely eliminate the population in succeeding years.

...Try and not keep picking in the same area. Vary the location in order to lessen your impacts.

...Do not pick from protected sites - sites of special scientific interest (SSSI).

...Yanking stalks from plants can damage them and encourage disease, so try and cut them.

...If you cannot clearly and unequivocally identify something, don't eat it.

...Consider potential hazards (not just physical e.g. falling in a ditch or cuts from thorns) but also from pollution.

...One must be careful not to pick watercress from stagnant pools and water which flows through sheep pastures as this could be dangerous. It has to be washed very thoroughly before eating. (The danger here is liver fluke.)

...Before going on to private property, it's a good idea to ask permission to do so.

...Always close gates after you.

Remember, that we should be handing on to future generations, a world that is richer than the one we inherited.

— ACKNOWLEDGEMENTS —

An expression of deep gratitude must go to Sally McKenna, for her generous and insightful new Introduction to this edition of *Wild and Free.* She and her husband John are Ireland's leading food critics. Their highly respected food guides have become the definitive word on where to find the very best of Irish food.

Sincerest thanks to the well-known expert on the medicinal value of wild herbs and plants, Vivienne Campbell, from the Scottish island of Bute and who now lives in Clare. She contacted me out of the blue when I was thinking of whether I should go ahead and republish and mentioned, that when giving a talk and demonstration at a Health Fair in Dublin in 2011, an attendee had described copies of the original as being like 'gold dust'! Thank you Vivienne, for your enthusiasm and a belief that *Wild and Free: Cooking from Nature* should be republished.

To Sorcha Sheerin, the best proof reader you could ever find - thanks too, Sorcha, for your pertinent comments and invaluable advice on the text.

A special word of thanks to Vincent Casey for his help in bringing this book to fruition.

I thank all those who have helped me with their advice, stimulation and friendship and were there for me whenever I needed them.

— SAFETY DISCLAIMER —

PREFACE

For many of us, the word foraging may conjure up almost forgotten memories of blackberry picking time, which was an event on the calendar year, almost as significant as that of Christmas or Easter. Over thirty years since *Wild and Free: Cooking from Nature* was first published in 1978, foraging for wild fruits, berries, greens, seaweeds and flowers has struck a chord with people today, who are now interested in the cooking of wild food. Apart from the outdoor enjoyment of searching and picking, it is important to note that wild food isn't an end in itself but that it is something we can integrate into our existing food sourcing and preparation to add diversity and a distinctive flavour to our diet.

I have been helped enormously on the road to republish by the numerous people who approached me to do so, especially of the younger generation, friends of my sons' who had heard their parents talk about the original publication. This was very heartening, as throughout most of the world wild food foraging is a way of life that has been handed down from generation to generation. Much of that changed with the growth of post World War11 agribusiness and the coming of the boom in the convenience food business of the 1950s. In the process people found that they could eat quickly and cheaply with little regard to food sources and quality. Wild food is growing in abundance all around us on hedgerows and hillsides free for the taking, but the wild food knowledge and skills that our not not-so-distant ancestors cherished, have all but disappeared. Many of the foods called 'weeds' e.g. nettles, dandelions, fat hen, prashock etc., and on which people today spend billions trying to eradicate, they saw as wholesome, healthy and very edible.

A great majority of our recipes were taken direct from our personal record book where they were jotted down over the years, more or less as we had proceeded. We didn't make a fetish out of our cooking, being like the mother-in-law who explains to her new daughter that when she is baking bread she uses 'two or three handfuls of flour, a pinch of salt, etc'. We did not believe that one should be over particular with quantities at the beginning but that an accurate record of the quantities should be kept so that as you gain more experience you arrive at the flavours, the strengths etc. which you personally prefer.

I dedicate this edition to the memory of my late husband, Cyril, poet, artist, scholar and environmentalist and to my two sons, Tadhg and Eoghan.

Kit Ó Céirín
Lisdoonvarna, 2013

NEW INTRODUCTION

by Sally McKenna

Anyone looking up at the stars in the sky might well be intimidated by their countless number. But thanks to the ancients, who came up with the concept of the celestial sphere, an imagined radius that became a practical tool for grouping the constellations, we now have a map. Beginning with the North Star and the Plough, we can gradually plot the stars, and what seemed huge and unquantifiable can easily be broken down into about twenty groupings that offer an easy solution to understanding and knowing what shines above us.

Likewise the ancients have grouped plants into families, so that, while at first it might not seem apparent, we can know that the bramble, the hawthorn and the meadowsweet are all actually part of the same rose family, and we can therefore make the presumption that they are all edible. Likewise we learn to distrust members of the buttercup family, which contains some of the most poisonous plants, or be wary of the umbellifers, a family that has both edible, and dangerous, members.

It is for this quantifying, mapping, describing and grouping that we owe so much to the foragers who have gone before us. And amongst this group of pioneers we must certainly be grateful to Cyril and Kit Ó Céirín.

First published in 1978, "Wild and Free" set out to interpret the wild for the casual enthusiast. Cyril and Kit's genius was to break the huge, seemingly unquantifiable world of nature into 22 easily recognisable sources. Just like the ancient astronomers who opened up the skies for us, "Wild and Free" gave us a focus for the plants that grow under our feet and, in doing so, made them available to us for nourishment and enjoyment.

It is a joy to see "Wild and Free" republished. We live in a different era from the late nineteen-seventies. These foods are now fashionable and recognised for their dietary significance. There are now many voices singing the praises of wild food.

One thing we share with the Seventies is that our values have re-aligned, and we are again in a time where the economic importance to the household of these foods is once again valued. And recent research has lead to unprecedented respect for the hunted and foraged foods of our ancestors. We now realise the nutritional importance of the buds, leaves, bark and roots that grow un-hybridised in nature.

Foraged food, meaning food collected from the wild, has always been a part of our diet. But we now understand that the ancient foragers who were our distant ancestors were actually eating for optimum health.

The diet of these hunter gatherers, we now know, exceeds our modern recommended daily requirement of vitamins and minerals between two and ten fold. Foraged food is recognised to be nutritionally richer than any of our modern day health diets. And, just like wood that heats you three times as you cut, chop and burn it, so foraged food nourishes repeatedly, as you study, search and cook with it.

But there is a further twist to the story of this book. Like any age, we worry today about losing what we know, both the skills and the stories. "Wild and Free" does more than just list the foods: it speaks of their place in our landscape and our culture. It tells the story of the blackthorn stick, the "true cross" superstitions of the elder, and the ear-like fungus "Judas Ears" that grows upon its scaly trunk. Kit and Cyril reference Celtic mythological legends in the story of the crab apple, or the story of the poor man who courted a widow's daughter and the stirabout of prashock that was offered, only to be substituted for potatoes and butter when a better suitor arrived on the scene.

To this manifold of information is added a further blessing in the wonderful, clear, precise illustrations of Cyril Ó Céirín. This is an empowering book, a book that illustrates, interprets, groups and documents, and it does all this for the lay person, the cook or gardener who wants information and nourishment from what lies abundantly around us.

The Ó Céiríns' sense of enquiry demystifies these foods, whilst at the same time adding to their mythology.

Sally McKenna
29 January 2013

...Trees of apples, huge and magic,
great its graces;
Crop in fistfuls from clustered hazel,
green and branching.

Sparkling wells and water-torrents,
best for drinking,
green privet there and bird-cherry
and yew-berries...

Eggs in clutches and God gives mast,
honey, heath-pease;
sweet the apples and the berries
of bog and heather.

A cup of mead from noble hazel,
swift the service;
acorns brown, bramble tresses
and their berries.

Then in summer pleasant mantle
of tasty savour;
marjoram, earth-nuts, and the tresses
of the streamlet...

7th century hermit poem, translated by James Carney

INTRODUCTION

Last year millions of pounds worth of fruit, free for the taking, was left to wither on the trees in Britain and Ireland. £2 million worth of *one variety alone* was disregarded in Ireland; the figure is based on the international market price and it represents the value of the estimated 20,000 tonnes of rosehips, a common, wild, indigenous fruit, which the Irish neglect to garner each year. In the north of England, however, prodigious quantities of the fruit are collected by casual labour and it is the one completely wild fruit which forms the basis of a British commercial enterprise - the production of rosehip syrup. On the other hand, there are a number of other unheeded wild fruits and flowers which already are or could soon be in demand commercially, but so far no one has dared to even attempt to calculate their potential value. These rather startling facts are only some of many surprises (most of the others, we hasten to assure you, are much more palatable) in store for the person who is beginning to take an interest in the hedgerow harvest of Ireland and the United Kingdom.

There are several hundred edible plants and fruits and fungi growing wild in these islands. Some are plentiful, some scarce, others plentiful but local. To become familiar with them all would require application in study, a great deal of travel for the purpose of fieldwork and – let's face it – the determination of an ascetic to regularly forego one's favourite foods in the interest of first-hand information. Not a few very fine field guides and comprehensive studies have been published which would be essential reading for anyone intending to pursue such a course. However, our own happy experiences with the wild harvest have led us to compile what we hope is a practical book for those who are not among the chosen few who have both the time and opportunity to absorb more than a sound working knowledge of nature's produce.

This book is, in the main, for those who have neither the energy nor desire to become experts in the whole field; for the ordinary person tied to a nine-to-five routine or to the kitchen sink; for the farmer and his helpmate whose 'work is never done'; for all those whose knowledge of the subject may be limited to a vague memory of 'what Granny used to do'. The book, in fact, is not only for these but is written by such as these. We, therefore, have concentrated on twenty-two of the more common and easily recognisable species, those most associated with tradition: blackberries and crab apples, of course;

field mushrooms and hazel nuts; dandelions once greatly prized, and nettles, for long an important subsistence and a staff of life; and others no more (or no less) exotic.

Many people will already know something about several of the species treated here; a lot of people probably are no strangers to the majority of them. Probably their surprise will initially spring from a renewal of acquaintance with things they had more or less forgotten. What we are willing to wager on, however, is that comparatively few have realised to what extent the harvest may be used. Take the common wild nettle, for instance: we couldn't fail to notice how surprised so many of our friends are when we enthuse over the virtues of this much-maligned and most useful plant. Yet, if our readers were born before the end of World War Two, most of them would soon recall that they have either eaten nettles themselves when young or seen or heard of others doing so. In fact, one of the remarkable aspects of the whole business is that it was not, as we had been led to believe, in the last century that people in general effectually turned their backs on the wild harvest but sometime within the past thirty to seventy-five years. This we are sure is true for a large part of Ireland at any rate, and also for the islands of Britain; we suspect that it is also true for a surprisingly large part of the British mainland itself. It is true, of course, that the decline in use and, therefore, in knowledge had begun a long time before.

There were several reasons for the change in eating habits. Obviously, the Industrial Revolution which incarcerated huge numbers of peasants and cottiers in the cities cannot be discounted. Of far greater significance was the corresponding revolution in land systems and farming methods. Who, for instance, would scout round for *praiseach* or charlock when there was a little garden of cabbage behind the cottage? Add to that the fact that, as more and more ground was enclosed and brought under the plough, the former abundance of herbs and fruits was no longer possible. There were other reasons. A study in depth would also have to take population increases into consideration and, say, the new systems of schooling. (Anybody who does not think the latter could have been of much import should recall Dickens's *Hard Times*.)

The last century and a half has brought about a remarkable change in eating habits, the decrease in the use of the wild harvest being only one significant aspect. It is no great exaggeration to say that the rate and extent of the change was caused as much by social notions as by economic notions. After all, this was the Age of Progress, the age of Dickens's Mr. Gradgrind. People chose to turn away from certain kinds of food (among them, of course, wild foods) because, for one reason or another, they associated them with inferior social status ('lower class') and poverty. This inferiority complex was nowhere nearly as great on the Continent as in Britain; nowhere in Britain was the sense of inferiority as destructive as in Ireland. Consequently, probably no people take less interest in the wild harvest than the Irish. In recent times at any rate, the British have shown far better sense – but then, the lessons of the last world war have not been lost on them. There has been a recent surge of interest, especially among the English. (We noted with approval recently that Queen Elizabeth had christened a £100 million Navy cruiser, the *Invincible*, with a bottle of home-made elderberry wine!) Indeed, it is a fair bet that, with typical thoroughness, the English will soon be making more use of nature's bounty than any people on the Continent. We feel this is wholesome. (Conservationists need not feel alarmed; as Richard Mabey in his fine book *Food for Free*, Collins 1972, has significantly remarked, 'no one is going to stand by whilst the hedge which provides his sloe gin is bulldozed down'.) Yet it is not all that easy – especially in this cynical and materialistic age – to show cause for thinking it wholesome. Certainly, we do not want to put the clock back nor do we advocate a Thoreau-like return to nature. We do not intend to argue that wild food is necessarily any more nutritious than cultivated produce, although such a stand might well be supported by facts such as the common weed, fat hen or *praiseach bhráthar*, containing more iron and protein than spinach or cabbage. Nor do we intend to argue that it is any more wholesome, even though it is not easy to keep away from the thorny ground of such a controversy when one has considered the question of herbicides and insecticides, artificial manures and weed-killers, not to speak of plant-breeding with commercial aims in view which just do *not* include food value or flavour.

There has been a good deal of talk of late about future shortages of seed and of the centralisation of food production, but far be it from us in this book to prophesise a doomsday situation. We could paint a picture of the truly remarkable concentration and energy with which the British (the British especially) and the Germans turned to the wild harvest during the last war, but the book – although it would be much more of a help than a hindrance – is not intended as a textbook for survival in times of future scarcity. We could (honestly) say that we are grieved that such a large body of popular information and experience is all but lost, yet we would be silly to think that a book which concentrates on twenty-two common species might of itself be of any great consequence in the recapture of such knowledge. Besides, neither of us lay any claim to being experts in this or any other related field. We have stated our belief that this is a practical handbook and therefore, albeit somewhat under protest, we allude to pounds and pence. We did not wish to dwell over-much on this point because it is not the most important point; yet, in this age of rising prices, we would not have shown common sense if we had ignored it. Wild food is free for the taking – that goes without saying – but, on the other hand, time has to be spent in harvesting it. Saving there is, of course, but how much depends on the individual. If you feel that there could be no significant saving involved, try saying the same to the suburban housewife who has just trekked all the way to supermarket X because she has made it her business to know that tea or lettuce or what-have-you is better value for money there than in supermarket Y. Two examples from our own experience should help to indicate comparisons: jam from wild fruit costs less by two thirds than ordinary jam in the supermarkets; a bottle of truly excellent elderflower wine was produced at less expense than a bottle of cheap, cooking sherry. More important is the fact that you know for certain what has gone into the homemade product.

There is a growing awareness of the economic potential of our wild harvest. For instance in 1973, *Concern*, an Irish organisation founded to assist the Third World, encouraged thousands of schoolchildren to harvest rosehips for this purpose. The hip (the fruit of the wild dog-rose) contains more Vitamin C than any other fruit or vegetable – twenty times as much as oranges, incredible though it may seem, and four times as much as the blackcurrants which form the basis of so many commercial Vitamin C tonics. In 1974, hips were selling at £100 a tonne. Irish schoolchildren had collected 25 tonnes of hips in the Autumn of 1973 and we took a little patriotic pride in this until we learned that, ten years previously, *one* school in England collected a staggering 14 tonnes, which, to aid some school project, they sold at a few pence per kilo, to a commercial manufacturer. As we have mentioned earlier, it has been estimated that last winter the Irish left some 20,000 tonnes of hips – a potential bonanza of £2 million – on the bushes. The implications of this one fact could afford enough food for thought to justify a White Paper on Education – for basically the matter is an educational one. A survey in a large Limerick City secondary school, a third of whose students are drawn from rural areas, uncovered the uncongenial information that only one child in twenty had ever – to their knowledge – seen a rosehip.

The general population of Britain may be only marginally less ignorant at the present but, at least, there the hip supports a national commercial industry, the production and export of rosehip syrup. During World War Two, the British Ministries of Health and Supply, using the County Herb Committees which had been founded and schooled as part of the 'war effort', had been garnering between 400 and 500 tonnes of hips a year. The opportunity of producing rosehip syrup commercially in peacetime was not lost. The fruit is collected each winter by casual labour and especially by groups of schoolchildren and by youth clubs.

In this handbook, we are concentrating in the main on kitchen larder and wine cellar, while taking care not to overlook altogether the therapeutic, educational and reflective aspects of the adventure (which undoubtedly emanate from it as mysticism does from yoga); yet, as it seemed to us that many people have been led to require an economic justification of one kind or another for any hitherto unaccustomed pursuit, we thought it no great harm to dwell a little longer on the commercial potential of the wild harvest. Take elderberries, for instance. Just how many thousand tonnes of this delicious and nutritious fruit might be harvested in Ireland and the United Kingdom during a good year is anybody's guess. The elder is one of the more common shrubs in these islands, far more plentiful than the dog-rose. It is so profuse in Co. Limerick, where we live, that the whole face of the countryside is transformed for the few weeks in midsummer when the flower is in bloom. Yet we have the preposterous situation in which Irish and British fruit juice-processing industries import huge quantities of the produce of the elder from countries such as Portugal and Czechoslovakia.

The dandelion is one of the most profuse of weeds in these islands and in late spring and early summer its gaudy yellow flowers are everywhere, even sprouting from cracks in concrete paths and from tarmacadam drives. In recent times, a Japanese firm let it be known that it would pay handsomely for Irish dandelions. Needless to say, no shipment left Ireland for Japan. On the other hand, a Scots family-firm exports substantial quantities of dandelion essence (what is commonly known as 'dandelion coffee') to the U.S.A. and to Australia.

Gaelic literature (the oldest vernacular literature in Europe) abounds from the earliest times with references to the hazel nut. Before the advent of the potato, hazel nuts had provided a major source of food. Even as late as the beginning of the nineteenth century, the itinerant poet Raifterí could hardly make a ballad in praise of an area without referring to its nuts – and he composed very many such pieces. The hazel still abounds despite the intervening agricultural revolution, land wars and bulldozers. Its proliferation is such in some areas that farmers long ago have given up the struggle to prevent it encroaching on what was once grassland. A laudable intention by a semi-state company to turn this proliferation to advantage in one such area, the Burren in Co. Clare, unfortunately was of no consequence. The immense sweet industries of Ireland and Britain still import all their hazelnuts. However, we have no axe to grind with regard to such large-scale commercial matters and our main reason for affording them so much space is merely to stimulate interest in the hedgerow harvest and to open the eyes of the uninitiated to the fact that it is still there, wild and free and abundant.

It is time for us to try to explain why we feel the revival of interest in nature's storehouse is wholesome. The medicinal quality of herbs has been authenticated, but this rightly belongs to a different, though related, field. Savings may well be substantial, but there is no pressing economic incentive. The valid enjoyment of wholesome food and good flavour is also under consideration, but these merely constitute the bait. We make the assertion that harvesting the wild is capable of being its own aim, object and end. The classic explanation for climbing a mountain holds good for this, too: because it is there. Wild food has to be found, its ways have got to be known, its acquisition demands that it be processed and put to its proper use. And it is herein that the seeds of wholesomeness are buried.

We are living in the 'age of the consumer', but man is, by nature, a producer, not a consumer. And life was meant for more than a succession of spirit-deadening routines. There is a real basis for the cliché, 'the lure of the outdoors' – who can recall blackberry-picking expeditions in childhood without recapturing some of the pleasure and the thrill? The renewing of contact with nature becomes an adventure and the deep running excitement and harmony that stems from it is something modern man especially must experience.

Bíonn an tEarrach ag saothrughadh 's ag síor-chur an tsíl,
Agus síleann sé fhéin gurab aige té 'n bhuaidh;
An Samhradh mar an gcéadna, ag cóiriughadh 's ag líonadh,
'S an Fóghmhar go faobhrach ag leagan le luas.

Spring, while he labours and sows seeds eternally, thinks that he only should bear the palm; Summer's the same as he furbishes and burgeons; and so, too, is brusque Autumn, dispensing in haste.
Séamus Dall Mac Cuarta (1647-1732)

part one

NATURE'S CALENDAR

THE FOUR SEASONS

This being a book about food and drink, not a medicinal handbook nor a general field guide to edible wild plants, the calendar below is necessarily limited to the two dozen or so species which we treat in detail. We had to fight hard to resist the temptation of including many more plants and fungi, so interesting or so useful are they in their own right. Among the criteria which governed the selection were: widespread distribution, easy recognition and harvesting, safety in eating and traditional usage. The calendar is based on our own experience in the south-west of Ireland. Obviously, plants will tend to be a little earlier in some parts (normally the more southerly parts of Ireland and Britain) than in others. Variations in weather conditions from year to year will also make for a certain inconstancy. Yet we believe that, no matter what the weather, the plants in actual fact do keep very closely to their expected timetables but when weather conditions are not the best the looked-for changes are less noticeable because they are less exuberant.

SPRING

Anois teacht an Earraigh, beidh an lá dul chun síneadh,
Is tar éis na Féil' Brighde árdóchad mo sheol,
Ó chuir mé im' cheann é ní stopfaidh mé choídhche
Go seasfaidh mé síos i lár Chonndae Mhuigheó.

Now with the coming of the Spring, the days will begin to stretch and after Brigid's Feastday I'll raise my sail; since I got it into my head I'll never stop until I stand down in the heart of the County Mayo.
Raifterí (1784-1835)

St. Brigid's Day (February 1st) is not only the first official day of spring in Ireland but also the day on which the farming communities ceremoniously hailed the spring by doing honour to their beloved saint. This was most appropriate (we have never come across a folk custom which was not, basically, appropriate) as one way or another Saint Brigid or Bride, as her name implies, is inextricably connected with the agricultural Mother Earth cult, with the earth-goddess, fruitful and bounteous, of whom Venus is merely a Mediterranean manifestation. Some archaeologists, indeed, hold that the pagan goddess and the Irish saint are one and the same thing; others, McAllister for instance, provoke even more interesting – and wonderful – thoughts on the relationship between Christian saint and pagan cult.

Whatever the facts are, the truths remain: man requires a ceremony so as to recognise and celebrate the bounty of Providence and glorify his Creator. This is probably even more true of man in vast urban sprawls and small town isolation than of his brethren in rural areas. Traditionally, part of St. Brigid's Day was given over to the planning of the year's work, a kind of public act of faith as it were. If you, because of your work or way of life, are in no position to 'observe' the first day of spring, might we suggest that you at least nod at Mother Earth by determining that this year you and your family will harvest some of her bounty. We say this a little hesitantly, for fear of being considered facetious; yet that we should be so aware of being considered facetious is surely indicative of the facetiousness of the life-style of this modern western world.

In *February*, is anything to be done? The snowdrops have heralded the end of winter for a month now, and solitary dandelions and, of course, daisies have made their challenge to the hard weather which can hit us anytime in January or February. If the weather is mild, you will be surprised at the number of dandelions: they are the true herald of the floral year. Still, you would cover a lot of ground if you had set out to make a few gallons of dandelion wine. It is the same with cowslips and primroses: spring begins in sheltered corners with these and with the dandelion which is soon so noticeable on roadsides. But there is normally too much labour involved with these, and they are still immature. Turn your attention to the lowly nettle; you can take the whole shoot now for your purposes, though traditionally it was not until later, about Easter, that people went through the process of blood-purification. And, by the end of the month, the *aiteann ghallda* or foreign furze should have really got down to the business of flowering. The sudden sleet, even, cannot extinguish its fire. Much of the countryside is all green and gold at this time, green fields with golden ditches (dikes, pardon us!) and you can take great sniffs of its heavy, honey scent as you set out to get the basis of your wine.

In *March*, it is mid-spring – and one of the few plants in Nature that does not seem to know it is the mistletoe, whose berries (although on the trees since Christmas) are just ripening about now. But this is of no interest to the beginner. Nettles and furze are. Collect flowers from the furze early on if you need them. The cowslip will surely surprise you early in the month, its crinkled leaves gathered in a rampart round the first fragrant, delicate flower; but now is hardly yet the time to gather them. You may be busy enough anyway with nettle beer and wine, dandelion beer and furze wine. Young prashock offers a beautiful, sweet vegetable for your table.

April is the month of the blackthorn, which, as the month progresses, seems to have every hedgerow sprinkled with snow; yet we know no one who makes wine from the flower. This is the time of the first cowslip seekers, the dandelion dalliers, the last of the foreign furze fanciers and the time when those very astute fathers, wishing to lead the family out on expedition on Fraughan Sunday, sensibly search among the heather for shrubby little plants with myrtle-like leaves and bell-shaped, pinkish flowers, the bilberry, now perhaps more noticeable than when fruiting. Cowslip and primrose adorn the fields and banks and dandelion is becoming abundant. Young hawthorn and beech leaves now go well in salads. Late spring is also the time to harvest carrageen. If the swallows come early, the dog rose will be a mass of pinks to greet them and the rowan and crabtree will hang out their bunting for the cuckoo. Tradition ascribes much use to the former (especially as a herbal medicine) and little to the rowan and crab flowers. To soothe your impatience, make beech leaf liqueur from the delicate, milky, translucent leaves. Summer is upon you anyway – and worth waiting for. Meanwhile, don't overlook the nettle or prashock...

SUMMER

Más tú chuireas i n-am, chan tú a chóirigheas an planda,
Bheir bláth ar na h-abhaillibh nó meas ar an gcraoibh,
Tóradh na talmhan a líonas an t-arbhar,
Bheir cnó ar na coilltibh nó aon dadaigh mar ghním.

Even though you, Spring, sow in time, it isn't you who dresses the plant or brings blossom on the crabtrees or mast on the branches, who fills the land's treasure-house with green corn or brings nuts to the woods, or who does anything such as I, the Summer, do.
Séamus Dall Mac Cuarta (1647-1732)

You are going to be busy, so we hope you have things well planned (even to taking your dandelion and cowslip before this, if plentiful). The sap has once more conquered frost and sleet and searing wind. Even though the fire of the furze is behind us, the typical colours of early summer come thick and fast and the air is heady with summer scents. Suddenly, too, whatever rain there is has softened and we are in a world of blossom. May is the reign of the may bush (also called whitethorn or hawthorn) which seems to be topped with thick whipped-cream – the may in flower is one of the most exhilarating sights of the year. No wonder the farmers brought it to the back door on May Day and the children decorated it with little posies of cowslips and primroses.

In *May*, hawthorn blossom wine was traditionally made. Cowslip ought still to abound. The dandelion is at its most plentiful – don't wait for June to pick it as its immense numbers seem to turn into puff-balls of seed almost overnight and, though it will flower throughout the summer, it soon becomes almost as solitary as in early spring. There will be enough in these three to keep you busy winemaking; you can safely leave meadowsweet alone until June, although it is now becoming conspicuous. The tops and young leaves of nettles are still edible by the way, and prashock, growing on the potato drills, will reward the tired weeder if he keeps some for his dinner.

In *June* the wild rose flowers in profusion, but this is not the best month for picking. Meadowsweet is coming into flower everywhere, it seems, in the early part of the month and you may try it for wine. Much better – possibly even the best of the wild and free wines – is that of the elderflower. Catch it in time: mid-June may have the trees laden with masses of creamy-white clusters and the air heavy with its muscatel-like scent, yet, by the beginning of the fourth week, the flowers are changing to great, flat-topped clumps of small, green fruits. The honeysuckle or woodbine is in flower and you may, if you feel like it, experiment with that for wine, too, but picking it in sufficient quantities is laborious. On the debit side, nettles are now too coarse to use, the cowslip and primrose fade rapidly and the dandelions, for the most part, have turned into 'clocks.'

July is the best month to pick rose petals (though they may have been in bloom for a month or more); they will surely all have gone by the end of the month and should be taken as the petals are being shed. If the weather is right – warm and humid – the mushrooms may be searched for with fair chance of reward. You will be fortunate if, having been unable to gather it in June, you still can find elderflower in good order. The native furze is coming into bloom – it will be better in August – and the meadowsweet is still with us.

Autumn is round the corner and its first fruit is the fraughan or bilberry: 'Fraughan Sunday' is the Sunday closest to the first day of autumn, either in July or August, so make all preparations for your expedition to the hills or bog.

AUTUMN

Tá mil a's drúcht a's féar ann súd,
Smólach, cuach a's céirseach,
I dtráth na Lúghnasa cnóa 'gus úbhla,
Áirní dubha a's sméara.

There's honey and dew and grass there, thrush, cuckoo and hen-blackbird, at harvest time there's nuts and apples, black sloes and blackberries.
Raifterí (1784-1835)

Early *August,* as well as being bilberry or fraughan time is also field mushroom time – and these may be found throughout the entire Autumn. Dulse is traditional eating at Lammas, too. The dwarf or native furze is at its best, probably, in this month. Meadowsweet is still with us in some abundance. As if the fraughans were a signal, other berries are appearing though most of them are not yet ripe enough for use. Blackberries may prove to be an exception, however, and so too may elderberries in kinder summers. Hazel nuts are plentiful, but may be somewhat too immature for most people's tastes; still it is interesting that the twenty second of the month is St. Philibert's Day and both he and his day are connected with nuts or 'philiberts'. Perversely, the fraughan season is just about over by the end of the month.

Early *September* still finds the native furze in bloom and you must keep a wary eye on the elderberries – when the clusters turn upside down, they're ready for picking – for, usually, the birds will have taken the best of them by the third week. And, of course, it is blackberry-picking time: how many people there must be who cherish memories of family expeditions after blackberries in their youth. 'Never pick blackberries after Ballyboggin Fair' the old folks used to warn us – and it is generally true that the berries are over-ripe around the date of the fair, the twenty-sixth. Never mind, this is probably the best time for hazel nuts and the haws may already be fat and soft enough to harvest. Crab apples, too, may be ripe enough for cooking. Certainly, dandelion roots are ready to dig up and the field mushroom ought to be still plentiful.

October, of course, finds the harvesting at its busiest. It is true that the black pods of the furze are 'popping' their seed and that the blackberry has lost its taste or turned fuzzy or 'has the maggot' (but don't forget that those at the end – not the tips! – of the branches may still be good enough for jams and jellies). The nuts, too, are being discarded and the haws, at their best probably in the first week, may be gone off by mid-month, or the missel thrush and other birds have fed greedily on the crop. It is a strange, paradoxical time, poised on the edge of winter, called in Irish 'the compensation of the year'. As the New Moon rises, the leaves are falling. And there is growth along with decay. Dying Nature is increasingly active, discharging its ordained duties. Few fading flowers so remarkably illustrate the cycle as the 'pop-gun' ploy of the furze, and the dramatic thud of a ripe crab apple, fallen from the branch, is our signal to harvest rosehips, sloes and wild plums. By mid-October, the sloes should have softened and their skins become permeable, the rose trees should blaze with ripe hips, the crabs and plums gleam with ripeness. You don't have to wait for the frost before taking perfect rowanberries; and, up to the onset of the cold, much may still flourish.

WINTER

My tidings for you: the stag bells,
Winter snows, summer is gone.

Wind high and cold, low the sun,
Short his course, sea running high.

Deep-red the bracken, its shape all gone –
The wild goose has raised his wonted cry.

Cold has caught the wings of birds;
Season of ice – these are my tidings.
Kuno Meyer (from the Old Irish)

Hallowe'en, which is Scotch for the Eve of All Saints, is in Gaelic, *Oíche Shamhna*, the feast of the dead. *Samhain fhuar an áir*, 'Cold November of the slaughter', it was termed and, as one looks at the bare, desolated trees, Armageddon comes to mind. At Hallowe'en, the old people believed the dreaded *púca* breathed on all fruit, poisoning them. But he must miss the crabs and plums and sloes, which may still be picked. (Don't forget to prepare your crabs for cider.) Otherwise it is no time for collecting wild fruits or flowers, though we have known a man make sloe gin late in *November* and enjoy it at the New Year festivities and have heard of another who made furze wine in winter. Whatever about the former, the latter we do not recommend.

December is the month in which cider making is traditionally begun, but otherwise winter's the time for reaping the fruits of your labours. A great deal of your wine made in the same year will be drinkable by Christmas. It will certainly give you a thrill – but don't get too carried away: remember it will improve still further as it matures. There are jams and jellies to gladden the heart and even give food for talk and thought. Sit down by your Yule log (even if it's an electric one), toast one and all in home-made wine or gin or liqueur and, when things quieten down, study this book... We hope it will whet your appetite and help gladden your heart without lightening your pocket.

MONTH BY MONTH AT A GLANCE

Remember that watercress is perennial and so may be gathered throughout the year; so too may dandelion, although the leaves are at their best in spring and the roots in autumn.

Month	What may be gathered	What may be made
FEB	Furze	Wine.
	Dandelion	Salad; soup; vegetable.
	Nettle	Broth; gruel; vegetable; beer; wine.
	Prashock/Charlock	Broth; gruel; vegetable.
MAR	Furze	Wine.
	Dandelion	Salad; soup; vegetable; beer.
	Nettle	Broth; gruel; vegetable; beer; wine.
	Prashock/Charlock	Broth; gruel; vegetable.
	Primrose	Syrup; tea.
APR	Furze	Wine.
	Dandelion	Salad; soup; vegetable; syrup; beer; wine.
	Nettle	Broth; gruel; beer; wine; vegetable.
	Prashock/Charlock	Broth; gruel; vegetable.
	Primrose	Syrup; tea; wine.
	Cowslip	Syrup; tea; wine.
	Hawthorn	Salad; tea.
	Beech	Salad; liqueur.
	Carrageen/Irish Moss	Desserts
MAY	Furze	Wine.
	Dandelion	Salad; soup; vegetable; syrup; beer; wine.
	Prashock/Charlock	Vegetable; gruel; broth.
	Primrose	Syrup; tea; wine.
	Cowslip	Syrup; tea; wine.
	Beech	Liqueur.
	Hawthorn/May	Salad; wine.
	Dulse	Salad; vegetable; 'laverbread'.
	Meadowsweet	Flavouring; tea; wine.
JUN	Furze	Wine.
	Prashock/Charlock	Vegetable; gruel; broth.
	Dulse	Salad; vegetable; 'laverbread'.
	Meadowsweet	Flavouring; tea; wine.
	Dog Rose	Flavouring; salad.
	Elder	Flavouring; thirst-quencher; wine.

JUL	Dulse	Salad; vegetable; 'laverbread'.
	Meadowsweet	Flavouring; tea; wine.
	Dog Rose	Flavouring; salad.
	Mushroom	Vegetable; relish; soup.
	Fraughan/Blueberry	Soup; desserts and pies; jam; jelly; thirst-quencher; wine.
AUG	Dulse	Salad; vegetable; 'laverbread'.
	Mushroom	Vegetable; relish; soup.
	Fraughan/Blueberry	Soup; desserts and pies; jam; jelly; thirst-quencher; wine.
	Furze	Wine.
SEP	Mushroom	Vegetable; relish; soup.
	Furze	Wine.
	Dandelion	Vegetable; 'coffee'.
	Elder	Chutney; soup; buns; pancakes; syrup; jams; thirst-quencher; wine.
	Hazel	Butter; cakes.
	Blackberry	Chutney; desserts, pies and tarts; syrup; jam; jelly; thirst-quencher; liqueur; wine.
	Crab Apple	Desserts; jelly; verjuice; cider; wine; thirst-quencher;
	Hawthorn	Jelly; wine.
	Rowan	Jelly; jam; wine.
OCT	Dandelion	Vegetable; 'coffee'.
	Hazel	Butter; cakes.
	Crab Apple	Desserts; verjuice; thirst-quencher; jelly; cider; wine.
	Hawthorn	Jelly; wine.
	Plum; Damson, etc.	Butter; desserts, tarts and pies; jams; wine.
	Rowan	Jelly; jam; wine.
	Blackthorn	Jelly; wine; liqueur.
	Dog Rose	Syrup; purée; jam; jelly; tea; wine.
NOV	Crab Apple	Desserts; jelly; verjuice; cider; wine; thirst-quencher.
	Plum; Damson, etc.	Butter; desserts, tarts and pies; jams; wine.
	Blackthorn	Jelly; wine; liqueur.
	Dog Rose	Syrup; purée; jam; jelly; tea; wine.

In December and January you may sit back and enjoy the fruits of your labours but, if you find yourself getting bored, you'll be glad you dried and bottled some of the harvest during the previous ten months!

Ba h-iomdha cnuastóir coille
De mhnáibh fionna na Féinne:
Agus caor de bhlas cúmhra,
Subhcraobh agus sméara,

Móineoga caomha corcra,
Biolar-fochain agus gleorádin –
Is na h-ingheana cas caol-fhion
Ba bhínn fuaim a n-órdháin.

Abundant was the harvest of the woods by the fair women of the Fianna: rowanberries with fragrant taste, raspberries and blackberries, sweet, purple bogberries, tender watercress and cow-parsnip – and the nimble girls slim and fair, sweet was the sound of their singing.
Ossianic Poem (17th cent.)

part two

GATHERING THE HARVEST

GATHERING THE HARVEST

Both by description and illustration, we have endeavoured to assist you to gather the harvest described by us. You should have no great difficulty with identification but, when unsure, it is best to consult a good field-guide. Remember also that among English-speakers the common names for identical plants may not only differ throughout the world but may also differ from county to county or even from parish to parish. Being a constant, the Latin name may prove to be very useful when looking up a field-guide or when cross-checking in a flora.

EQUIPMENT

When you actually set out on expedition to field or wood or moor, *do* come prepared. Children in bare legs will certainly fall prey to thorns and nettles; nothing is more likely to dampen the enthusiasm of any group, no matter how determined, than a child's wet feet. The answer is wellingtons – for all. Gloves are more than useful; let them be thin and, if possible, not woollen. Men will, doubtless, baulk at wearing them but it is something in the nature of a truism to comment that a female properly gloved will pick far more furze flowers and even rosehips or blackberries than a gloveless he-man.

People, especially children unused to the countryside, are going to get stung by nettles. Unless you rely (as we do) on spittle and bruised dock leaves, it would be wise to bring along some lotion. Some form of picking stick is necessary. Take a tip from the old Gaelic folk-saying *sméar mullaigh* – an epithet, applied to anything choice, in particular a scion of very good family, which translated literally means 'a berry from the top-most branch'. The choicest berries are generally on the higher parts of the tree, i.e. on those most exposed to the sunlight. A walking-stick with a crook is certainly a help; some people tie a wire coat-hanger to a light pole; we normally carry a very light garden rake. You will also require a sharp knife or a scissors – not so much for your own convenience as to minimise damage to plants. Although everybody used 'tilly cans' for carrying home blackberries when we were children, it is best to use non-metal containers. A flat, open basket is excellent. If you have to use plastic bags, do not exclude air for too long or the produce will 'heat' or go mouldy. A small, stout spade is essential if you are gathering roots.

HARVESTING

If you live in suburbia, go as far away as feasible from city or town or public highway when you bring the family harvesting. Otherwise the whole exercise is not only something akin to a lion-safari in a zoo but it is antisocial as well. You will never pick alongside busy roads if you consider the obvious contamination from exhaust fumes, dust, splashes and, possibly, weed-killers. Keep a wary eye open for places which may have been treated with weed-killer or have had insecticide spray blown on them by the wind. The golden rule is to pick only that which looks choice and fresh and with no signs of decay or damage, insect or otherwise. In case we have frightened you off a little, let's put this whole business into perspective: the chances are that a great deal of the food you use at the present has undergone treatment with chemicals.

It is desirable to harvest when fruit, etc., is dry, as otherwise it is quick to mildew. Morning is often the best time as a day of strong sunshine diminishes natural oils in the produce. When gathering flowers, follow the example of the bees who will be at their most industrious when flowers are at their best. In general, herbs and leaves are best gathered in the spring; but if you are going to dry them, pick them just as the plant is beginning to come into flower. (Use a scissors and leave as much stalk and leaf as possible on the plant.) Lay them carefully in their container as they will tend to spoil if crushed in a bag. Roots are in finest condition in the Autumn; be careful not to damage them when lifting and brush off as much earth as possible on the spot. Remember, too, that every root lifted is a plant *and* its future progeny is eliminated, so never pick more than you require. (The only root we have mentioned in the recipes is that of the dandelion, a herb which is still, thank goodness, very common.) Fruit should be ripe, of course, but not over-ripe or damaged, though windfall apples may be used.

The gathering of mushrooms, hazel nuts and watercress is treated in the sections which specifically deal with these. Never pick more than you can use immediately. The saying in Gaelic, *Is fearr leath ná meath,* holds good: a small amount put to good use is better than a large amount going bad. In general, pick less than you think you'll need. Never strip a plant or take large quantities of anything from the one shrub – it must be allowed to seed and multiply. We feel a little guilty about the section on cowslips and primroses in this book; only the fact that they were once very widely used in the kitchen (especially in England) prompted us to include it at all. By all accounts these flowers have suffered greatly from over-picking in Britain. As regards the other plants mentioned, there would seem to be no cause for concern – at present at any rate. Yet, one never knows. Take nettles, for instance. One would hardly have any fears for them so proliferous and tenacious are they. Yet, the records of a Natural History Club in 1867 expressed concern over a possible shortage of nettles if people continued to eat them at the rate they were doing at that time.

PRESERVING BY DRYING

The drying of herbs, flowers and fruits requires no special equipment and the three most important ingredients for success are care, patience and experience.

When drying fruit, make sure it is not over-ripe or damaged. Wash and dry well in a cloth. Place in a single layer on a tray or toast-rack in a very cool oven – as low as 100°F (50°C) if possible. This will take up to six hours normally, but may take longer with bigger fruit such as plums unless you stone and halve them. The fruit may be judged to be dry if, when squeezed, no juice is apparent and the skin is wrinkled but not baked hard. Herbs and flowers may be dried out of doors, but it will take something in the nature of a heatwave to do so. Never leave them in direct sunshine (as this will reduce their goodness) but spread on wire trays or on a sheet of paper in the shade or hang in loose bunches (preferably in muslin bags) from the shaded under-branches of trees or bushes. It is better, perhaps, to put them into a well-ventilated shed or garage (a greenhouse will often be found to be too humid). Some people will dry them in the oven as for fruit but the combination of gentle heat, good ventilation and convenience is just as often found in kitchen or airing cupboard. Always place on a sheet of paper or wire tray or, better again, hang loosely bunched in muslin bags. Above all, make sure that air can circulate freely around the herbs or flowers and that the atmosphere is dry. Some people like to give them a 'boost' in the oven for an hour or so first of all. It will take anything from a week to three weeks to dry the produce. Turn often and rearrange the leaves or petals on their rack. When the whole is dry enough to enable crushing with a rolling pin, it is ready. Crush as finely as possible, pack in air-tight glass or earthenware jars and store in a dry, dark cupboard. If your dried herbs tend to lack flavour or colour, it may be that, if oven-dried, too much heat was used. On the other hand, perhaps they were harvested when past their prime; it is always best to pick from young plants. The drying of mushrooms and hazelnuts is treated in the articles dealing specifically with these items.

part three

UTILISING THE HARVEST

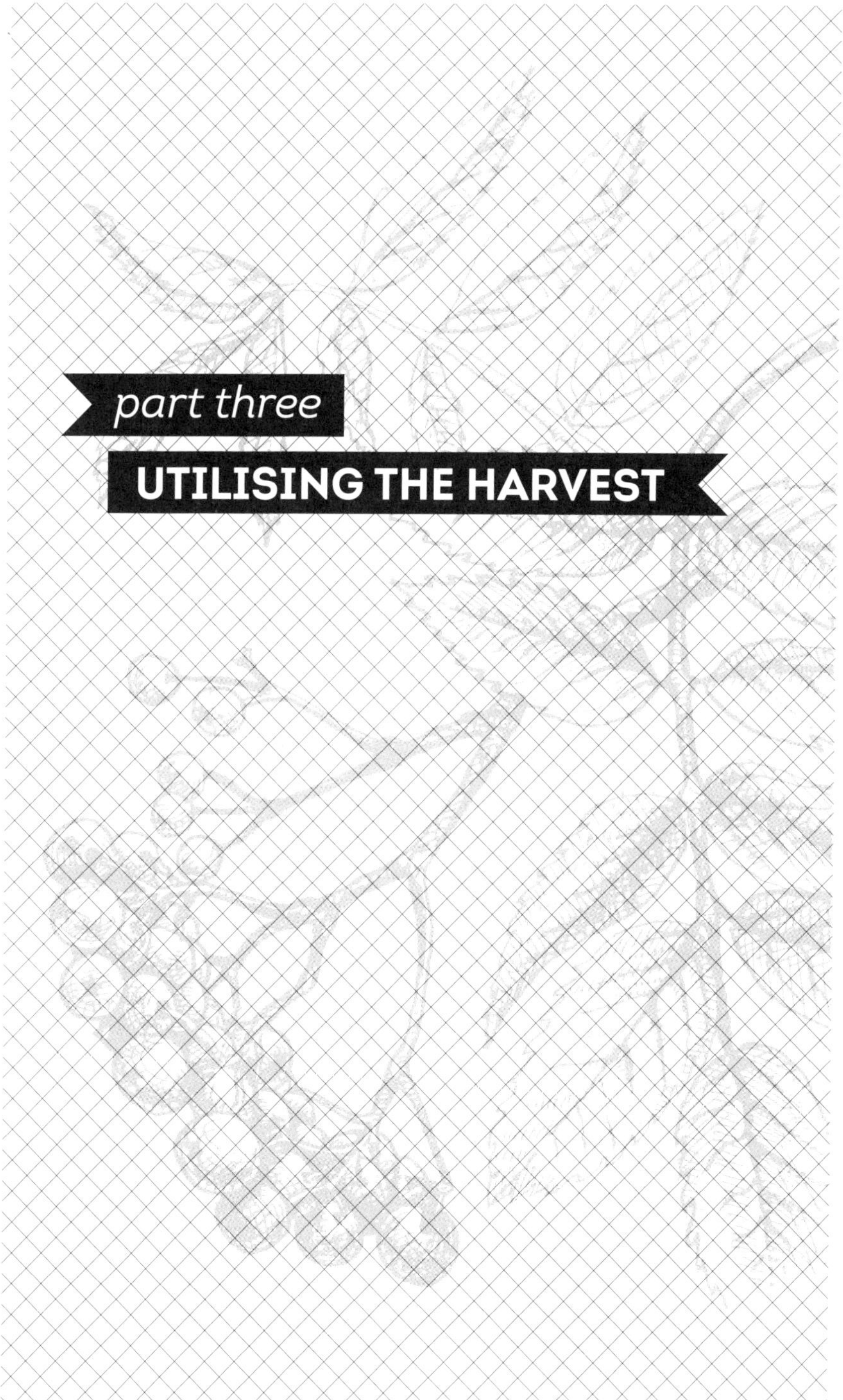

UTILISING THE HARVEST

As our cultivated vegetables and fruit are descended from indigenous or foreign weeds, there is nothing mysterious about the cooking of the wild harvest. We make ordinary Indian tea by putting the dried leaves into a pot and pouring on boiling water, why shouldn't we do the same when making other herbal teas? The basic principles of jam-making apply whether the basis is apricot or fraughan. If nettles or prashock are to be used as a vegetable, there is no need to treat them differently from the more ordinary greens. And a salad, you might say, is a salad. Therefore, while we have included over one hundred recipes and detailed instructions on the making of jam, jelly and wine, etc., it would have been outside our scope to have produced anything that smacked of a comprehensive cookery book. Many of the recipes are chosen to open the eyes of those inexperienced in or doubtful of the uses to which the wild harvest may be put and the rest are intended merely as guides. Do not be afraid to experiment or to trust your own judgement as to what best might suit your own tastes. In other words, our recipe sections are intended to complement a good cookery book. Most of the recipes represent the way we normally utilise the harvest (which explains some seeming anomalies – for example, although we give a reasonably detailed description of one method of wine making in this chapter, recipes may not always adhere rigidly to this guide). Some of the methods came from friends and relations, others we gleaned from living tradition and a few are our interpretation of instructions found in very old books; still others are common knowledge.

SALADS

Of the species mentioned in this book, the following are recommended for use in salads: young beech leaves, young hawthorn leaves and dandelion leaves, watercress, elderflowers and dog rose petals, dulse, and hazel nuts.

VEGETABLES

Nettles and prashock were the most commonly used as vegetables among the plants treated here; watercress, too, was stewed and dandelion root used to be very popular in parts of England, especially; both carrageen moss and dulse may also provide novel tastes as vegetables to non-coast dwellers. Wild greens may be cooked in the same way as garden spinach. Other old-fashioned ways of treating nettles and prashock are given in some detail in their respective sections, and they may also be included in traditional dishes such as champ, colcannon or coddle.

SOUPS

We have gone into some detail as regards the fine soups made from nettles and prashock but, of course, there is nothing new about mushroom soup while many coast dwellers will surely think dulse in fish soup no novelty. On the other hand, sweet soups with a soft fruit base are not as common in these islands as they ought to be. Sweetening is less than would be used when preparing a dessert dish and the soup may be served hot or chilled. Enamel saucepans are recommended for cooking fruit soups. We have included a recipe for fraughan soup while an acquaintance of ours, a naturalist, has recommended haw soup to us.

SWEETS AND DESSERTS

There is such a variety of ways in which to approach the making of desserts that we can only repeat our earlier advice about utilising wild food: use your cookery book(s) *and* your imagination. However, we have included several recipes in their appropriate sections as a pointer. On the other hand, only a surfeit makes us progress from the time-honoured plate of fresh soft fruits, cream and sugar. Some soft fruits, especially blackberries, may be soaked overnight in the corresponding home-made wine or the juice may be collected after straining through a jelly bag, allowed to stand for a few hours in a warm atmosphere and eaten with cream.

A basic method for using flowers in earlier times merely called for simmering for a short while before cutting small and mixing in cream or milk and honey. Flowers of course, especially elderflowers and meadowsweet, are most easily used as a flavouring.

SYRUPS

We find this one of the easiest ways of preserving wild foods. Syrup may be used as a basis for soft drinks (i.e. mixed with water, soda-water, milk) or poured over desserts or spread on scones or bread (with or without butter or margarine).

When using fruit, let it be soft, over-ripe even (but not unwholesome). For fear of burning it is best to cook it in a covered earthenware bowl or pyrex jar which is placed in a saucepan of boiling water. Ideally, perhaps, water ought not to be added to the fruit but, in practice, up to half a pint (300 ml) of water per 1 lb (500 g) of fruit is used. Go easy with the water when dealing with the softer fruits – fraughans, for instance, will hardly require any water at all. Cook until soft, crush with a wooden spoon and strain in a good jelly bag, overnight preferably. We normally add 1 lb (500 g) of sugar per pint (600 ml) of juice but some people prefer a good deal less, especially if they are to use the syrup undiluted. Stir thoroughly to dissolve and, if you require quite thick syrup, boil rapidly for five minutes. Pour into warmed jars or bottles; we find Kilner jars excellent for larger amounts, screw-topped mineral-water bottles just right for smaller amounts (especially for flower syrups, as their harvesting is often laborious). Sterilize by placing lidded containers in a saucepan of boiling water, making sure jars do not touch each other or the bottom of the saucepan for fear of breakage, and simmer for a half hour or so. Store in a cool, dark place and it will keep from one season through to the next. As for flower syrups, use 1 pint (600 ml) of water per 1 lb (500 g) of flowers. Pour the boiling water over the flowers and leave them to steep for twenty-four hours. Strain, add 1 lb (500 g) of sugar per pint (600 ml) of juice, bring to the boil gently until the liquid attains the consistency of syrup. Bottle and sterilize as above. Note: before tackling rosehip syrup, read the specific instructions carefully.

JAM MAKING

Basically, jam is made by simmering fruit in a little water to break it up into a pulp and by then adding sugar and boiling the mixture to make it set and to preserve it. For preference the jam should be made on the day you pick the fruit. You cannot produce good jam unless you use fruit that is sound and not over-ripe. Under-ripe fruit is rich in pectin, the natural substance that makes jam set; ripe fruit, of course, has more flavour. If acid is present it helps extract the pectin. Some fruits have both pectin and acid, some are deficient in one or the other. This is why we often mix two fruits in making jams and jellies: crab apple and elderberry, plum and crab apple etc. Otherwise lemon (juice of 1 lemon to 2lb (1 kg) fruit) is added.

Fruits should be washed or, in the case of soft berries, wiped gently with a tea cloth. Remove stalks and leaves, and peel and core apples. Use a preserving pan or saucepan which is large enough to be only about half full when the pulp and sugar have been added together; this allows the rapid boiling which is necessary for a good set. A long-handled wooden spoon or, better still, a light but strong piece of wood about 1¼" (3 cm) in width will not only save you from a nasty burn or two but will also enable you to prevent the jam sticking to the bottom of the pan. Place the fruit in the saucepan with just enough water to cover; if the fruit is juicy use very little water. Bring the fruit to the boil and simmer slowly until it is very soft. Do not add the warmed sugar until the fruit has been reduced to a pulp as the sugar tends to harden the fruit. Remove jam from heat and add the sugar, stirring until it is all dissolved. Return to heat and boil rapidly until setting point is reached. The quicker this point is reached the better the jam will be – over-boiling takes both from the flavour and the set. Setting point is usually reached after ten minutes boiling. Two time honoured methods of testing for a set are foolproof with a little experience:

(1) Place a teaspoonful of the jam on a cold saucer and leave in a cool place (the window-sill for instance) until cold. Now push the jam with your finger – if it wrinkles, showing that a skin has formed, setting point has been reached. Don't be all day about this though or the jam may have over-boiled by the time you have finished and may have actually passed setting point.

(2) The other method is: lift the stirring spoon out of the jam and hold it horizontally, allowing the jam to drip off. If the drip is thick and heavy then the jam is done.

Remove from cooker and skim with a hot metal spoon. Allow the jam to cool before stirring and putting into heated jars. Fill to the brim and put on the waxed paper discs which help to exclude air. It is best to cover the jam as soon as possible, but otherwise do this when it is quite cold. Never cover when lukewarm. Unless you will be using unusually large quantities of jam at a time, it is better to store in 1 lb (500 g) jars than in the larger sizes. Experience proves that it is worth while labelling the jars with both name and date of making.

JELLY MAKING

When making fruit jellies, the basic rules for both selecting the fruit and producing the jelly are similar to those of jam making, except that you separate the juice from the fibres and other roughage by straining. There is therefore no need (except in the case of rosehips) to peel or core or even to remove flower-ends or small stalks, especially as these contain much pectin. Windfalls of crabs are excellent as long as the bad parts are cut away.

First the fruit must be reduced to a pulp. Place in a preserving pan and add just enough water to cover, remembering that when the fruit used is very juicy less water is required. Simmer until mushy but do not boil as you may reduce its capacity for setting.

It is at this stage, if the particular fruit you are using has a low pectin content (blackberries and fraughans, for instance), that pectin substitute must be added. We would prefer lemon juice (one lemon to every 2 lb (1kg) fruit) to the patent setting agents. However, from our own experience we recommend combining a fruit rich in pectin (such as crabs) with pectin-deficient fruits in the original ingredients. When the pulp is ready, strain through a jelly bag and allow to drip overnight for best results; squeezing the bag always forces some of the pulp through and the clarity of the jelly will be affected. Extra care must be taken at this point when straining rosehips. If you haven't got a fine jelly bag, a large square of flannel, or a few thicknesses of muslin will do. Line the container with the strainer, pour in the fruit pulp, lift, tying the corners of the improvised bag, and hang above the bowl. We find the handiest support for the jelly bag is from the handle of a drawer, the latter having been pulled out a few inches to provide a good overhang. Some people tie a doubled linen cloth to the legs of a kitchen chair and catch the juice beneath in a large bowl.

Measure the juice and bring to boiling point. Remove from heat. For each pint (600 ml) of juice allow 1 lb (500 g) sugar, which should always be warmed before adding. Stir the mixture until the sugar is completely dissolved. Return to cooker and boil rapidly for about ten minutes, then test for a set (see page 41, jam making). Skim jelly carefully if you want it to look clear and brilliant. A hot metal spoon will do the job best. Proceed as in jam making, except that Granny would probably have left the jellies to cool on a sunny window sill, as it was believed that this brought out the flavour. Unless you will be using unusually large quantities of jelly at a time, it is better to store in 1 lb (500 g) jars than in the larger sizes.

BOTTLING

Bottling, we must confess, is not a means of preserving wild fruit which we often practice. Not, we hasten to add, that we have anything against bottling but simply that we happen to have stuck for the most part to making jams, jellies and wines from fruit and syrups from flowers and we also make good use of our freezer. We are informed, however, by the home economist of a reputable, international manufacturer of bottling and preserving jars that most wild fruits could best be bottled in the same way as raspberries; however, we are led to believe that elderberries do not bottle satisfactorily. Many people, in fact, do bottle blackberries (just think of blackberry pie in mid-winter!) and there is no doubt that wild plums bottle excellently (we recommend that you halve and stone them). The golden rule is to choose fruit which is firm-ripe or indeed slightly under-ripe. It should be as fresh as possible, free from all blemishes and it may also be a help if it is even-sized. To prevent crab apples turning brown during preparation, keep after peeling in cold salted water, 1 tablespoon salt to 2 pints (1200 ml) of water, and of course rinse the fruit before packing into the bottles.

Remember that success depends on efficient sterilization and probably most people would agree that the Oven Method is ideal, being simple and requiring no additional equipment (apart from the preserving jars, of course). By all means, use your favourite method of bottling, if you have one. We would advise that the beginner use the proprietary brands of special jars (Kilner are excellent, for instance) or the patent covers which may be used with ordinary jam-jars. Unless you are bent on being absolutely self-sufficient and on making ultimate protests against waste and consumerism, we doubt if you will have much interest in the traditional method of sealing the (cooked) fruit in earthenware jars with mutton fat. Check that the rims of the jars are not chipped (as this might prevent a good seal) and that the rubber rings have not perished. Scrupulously wash your jars and rinse them but do not bother to dry them.

Fruit may be bottled in plain water if desired but will probably not have a full-bodied flavour. Preferably use sugar or honey or golden syrup as a sweetener: the strength of the syrup will depend on the sourness of the fruit and on your own individual taste. A usual guide is 8 oz (225 g) of sugar to 1 pint (600 ml) of water, which will give enough for four 1 lb (500 g) jars. Dissolve the sweetener in the water and simmer for a minute or two. Pack the fruit as closely as possible without squashing it up to within one inch of the rim and then – for Wet Pack – fill with the syrup (if using ordinary glass jars, the syrup must first be allowed to cool somewhat). Follow the manufacturer's instructions carefully as regards adjusting the lids or sealing rims; screwbands must *not* be put on at this stage.

Place several thicknesses of newspaper in a roasting pan or meat tin, or use a wooden board. Have the oven heated to the required temperature (see below) beforehand. Stand the jars in the roasting-pan or whatever, about 5 cm apart, and cook for the time given below. Remove the jars one at a time to a wooden surface and screw down screwbands tightly or fix clips, according to manufacturer's instructions. When the jars are cool (wait overnight if necessary), remove the band or clip and test for a successful seal by lifting each jar by the sealing disc alone. If a seal has been established, replace bands or clips. Label and date and store in a cool place. For Wet Pack, approximate 300°F (150°C), Gas Mark 1 will be required and soft fruits will take thirty to forty minutes, while plums and crabs will require fifteen minutes longer. (Some people prefer to use a slow oven, 200°F (95°C) Gas Mark ¼ for a couple of hours.) Soft fruits such as blackberries should be Dry Pack: do *not* fill the jars with syrup until after they have been removed from the oven. Brine, of course, is used instead of syrup with vegetables, using ½ oz (15 g) salt to 1 quart (1200 ml) water.

LIQUEURS

We hesitated to mention liqueurs at all as they are so expensive. Nevertheless, we felt that they could not be excluded as sloe gin is so traditional in so much of Britain and Ireland, and as the latter people, at least up to a couple of hundred years ago or less, made it a practice to flavour their ales, wines and spirits with herbs and wild fruits as do so many Continentals to this day. A special whiskey called *scáiltín* was flavoured with cinnamon and cloves and earlier still whiskey was sweetened with wild liquorice. An Elizabethan Englishman recorded that Irish whiskey or 'usquebaugh' was preferable to English 'aqua vitae' because of 'the mingling of raisins, fennel seed and other things.' What these 'other things' were is not hard to guess if we think of Continental home-flavoured spirits such as brännvin and schnaps: blackberries, fraughans, heather, cowslips, elderflower, elderberries, sloes, meadowsweet, etc. – in fact, most of the items treated in this book as well as caraway, thyme, tansy and many others. Earlier still, mead and metheglin were given the same treatment and, doubtless, wines were flavoured in much the same ways as have been recorded of the Gauls. The principle behind herb liqueurs is that the alcohol extracts the colour and flavour of the herb or fruit and a sweetening agent (originally honey, but usually sugar nowadays) is added. Equal weights of sugar and fruit are used. When using fruit, half-fill the bottle (screw-topped fruit-bottling jars make excellent containers) with the mixture of sugar and fruit, fill with the appropriate spirit, screw the lid on tightly and leave for a couple of months or more. Shake the jar and turn upside down once a week. Eventually, strain and bottle well.

When using flowers, press down well into the jar until most of it is filled and then top up with the spirit. Two to three weeks is usually enough to leave the infusion, stirring and turning upside down once or twice weekly. Strain. 1 lb (500 g) or ¾ lb sugar per pint (600 ml) liquor is dissolved in as little warm water as it takes to do so and a little extra spirit is added to this. Now mix well and bottle.

Of the species treated in this book, the following mixtures are or have been common: sloes and beech leaves in gin; blackberries, mayflowers and rose petals in brandy; meadowsweet leaves in mead; meadowsweet leaves and flowers of cowslip, primrose and rose in wines; rowanberry and furze flowers (it would seem) in whiskey. Elderflowers seem to go well with nearly everything and we found them well-mated with whiskey.

WINEMAKING

The way that people 'go on', you might be led to believe that you have to know as much as a chemist and possess a mini-laboratory to produce good wines. This is absolutely untrue. If you have the time, money and inclination (obsession may be a more correct term) you may go so far as to produce wines that ought to satisfy even the most fastidious of connoisseurs, but surely most of us merely wish to produce good, wholesome wines, cheaply and with the minimum of expense and time. Our aim in this section is to assist you to do just that. There is a great deal more to be learned on the subject than we give here and experience is the best of teachers. If you find yourself 'hooked' – on winemaking, we hasten to add – we suggest you study at least one of the many comprehensive books on the subject.

Strictly speaking, wine is the fermented juice of fresh grapes. For your home-made wines, however, you may use most edible wild fruits and a few wild flowers. Cultivated vegetables such as parsnip, turnip, carrot, beetroot and potatoes have also been much used, though more so in Britain than in Ireland. In fact, we have drunk excellent wine based on used tea-leaves, brewed each Christmas by nuns who keep an Old Folks Home! Indeed, the list of ingredients used in home winemaking seems endless. Probably, we can blame the Celts for the fact that no really strong tradition of wines made on a basis of our wild fruits has been established in these islands; they would seem to have found it easier to import wine from their home-lands than to develop the local fruits for the purpose of winemaking.

When choosing a basis for your wine, we suggest that, at the beginning, you stick to those ingredients traditionally preferred: apple, blackberry, elderberry, sloe, dandelion, cowslip and, especially, elderflower. Although we have come across very little reference to it in tradition, from personal experience we recommend haw wine. Furze, rowanberries and wild plums have also been much used in the past.

Equipment

Basically, all you need is a polythene bucket and a cloth to cover it, another cloth for straining, a small amount of cotton-wool or a fermentation lock, a wooden spoon, a vessel in which to ferment the wine, about three feet of quarter-inch rubber tubing for syphoning, and bottles. The handiest and cheapest fermentation vessels are the 1 gallon (4½ litres) glass jars, which may be obtained from wholesale grocers or home-winemakers suppliers. So you can see that, if you wish to experiment, you may do so without any special equipment. On the other hand, convinced that home-winemaking is for you, you could launch out and buy a few extra items: a nylon strainer, a more sophisticated syphon, wine bottles and new corks, a funnel, colander, lidded polythene bucket, a hand-corking machine and more fermentation locks. It will make things a lot easier if you have a barrel with both bung and tap. The traditional oak barrel is hard to come by these days (and, by the way, it involves extra work), but there are reasonably priced polythene barrels on the market.

If you have never seen a fermentation lock, you will be far less confused if you study the diagrams opposite of this essentially simple device. The idea behind the lock is that the carbon dioxide be allowed to escape but air is prevented from entering. The simplest type is made up of a glass or plastic tube in such a way that it can discharge the gas through water. The stem is pushed through the centre of the bored cork which fits firmly in the mouth of the jar or bunghole of the barrel. Some use a little water to prevent entry to air, but it is better to use a little sterilizing solution – the Campden fruit-preserving tablet so much associated with winemaking is commonly used, about a half tablet to a quarter cup of warm water. As for levels of liquid in the tube, the diagrams will guide you. It may be necessary to replenish this from time to time. By the way, the gas formed during fermentation will push the water or solution a little up the outlet side in that type of lock which has a U-shaped bend; when fermentation is finished, this will drop back level again.

A selection of four different types of fermentation traps (air-locks)

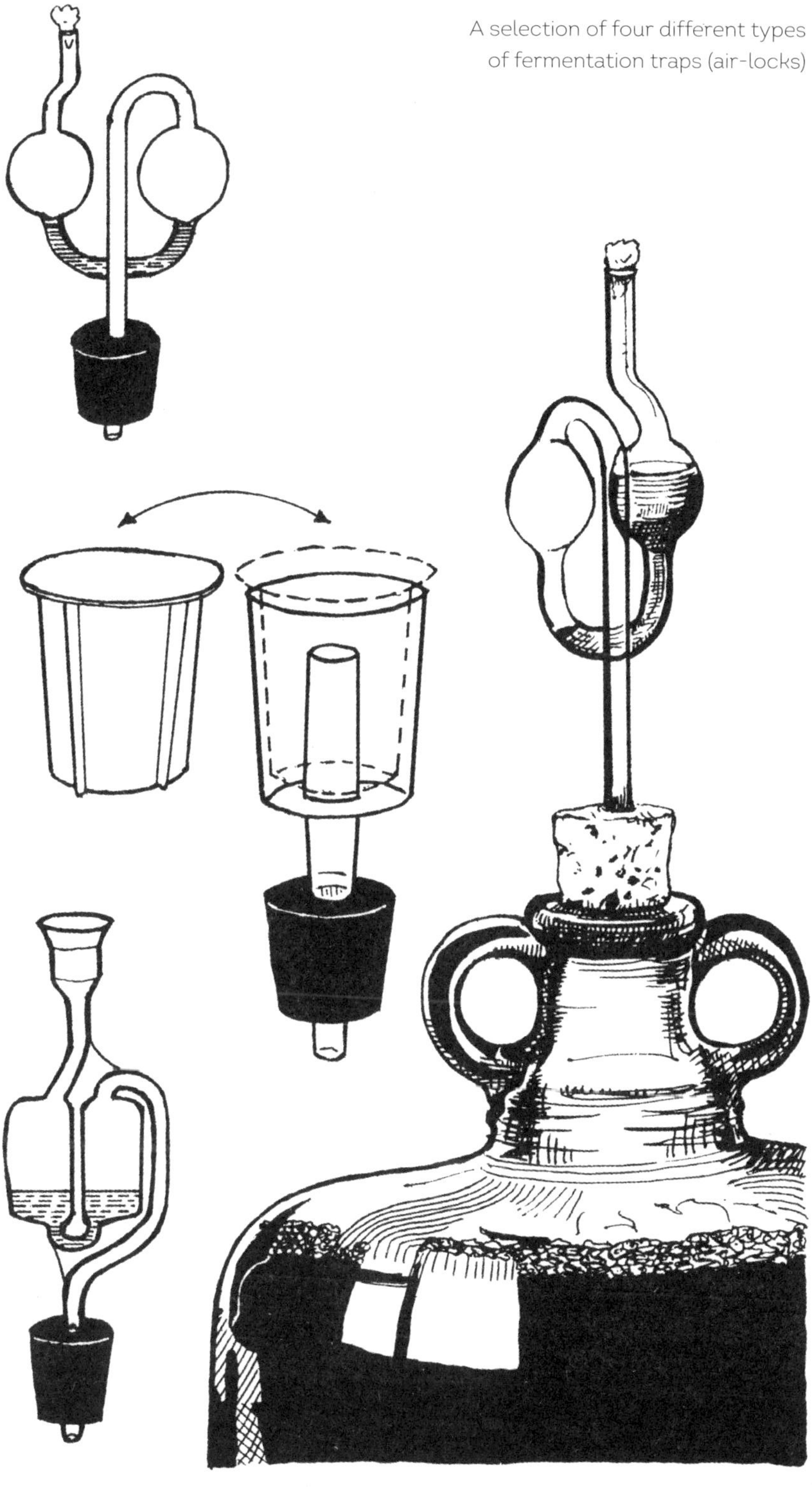

Making a Simple Country Wine

BLACKBERRY

CONTINUED —

5

KEEP IN WARM PLACE 65° TO 75° F. PLUG NECK WITH COTTON WOOL FOR A DAY OR SO. REPLACE WITH NEW COTTON WOOL IF STAINED BY FROTHING.

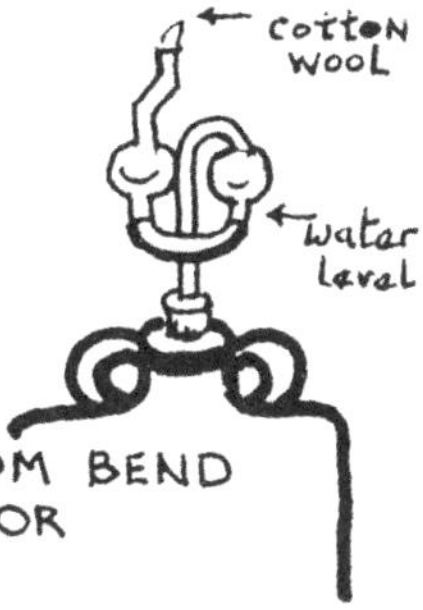

FIT TRAP
WHEN FROTH HAS SETTLED SOMEWHAT, FILLING BOTTOM BEND WITH WATER OR GLYCERINE.

6

WHEN WINE CLEARS, SYPHON (RACK). REPLACE TRAP, KEEP FERMENTING.

WHEN FERMENTATION IS OVER, SYPHON INTO STORAGE JAR. TOP UP WITH WINE OR BRANDY, OR MIXTURE OF 3 OZ. SUGAR TO ½ PINT WATER.
REMOVE TO **COOL** PLACE.

7

THE LONGER THE WINE IS KEPT IN BULK, THE BETTER. LEAVE AT LEAST 6 MONTHS TO MATURE.

ANY FURTHER SEDIMENT OR LEES MAY BE RACKED OFF WHEN SYPHONING INTO BOTTLES. (GIVE WINE A CHANCE TO CLEAR BEFORE YOU USE A CLEARING AGENT.)

8

USE WINEBOTTLE CORKS. A CORKING TOOL IS HANDY. OTHERWISE ...

In its simplest form, the syphon is a length of rubber tubing. One end is lowered into the container to a couple of inches above the sediment; a long darning needle put through the end of the tube will help you maintain this height or you may be able to clip the tube to the lip of the jar with a clothes peg. The other end hangs to a lower level outside so that the wine can flow into another container. By sucking it, you can begin the flow of wine. A more sophisticated syphon with push-button for stopping and starting may be bought; this is undoubtedly handier and saves much time. You must make sure that all your equipment is clean. Many experienced winemakers rinse theirs in a solution of sodium metabisulphate (Campden tablets) and then wash in clean water. Never use metal containers or even metal sieves or spoons.

As you become more expert, you may feel like adding other items to your stock, hydrometers for instance. But by that time anyway, you will have studied at least one book which is given over wholly to this almost inexhaustible subject.

Stage One: Preparing the Must

The process of winemaking is basically simple – after all, there are written references to it going back four thousand years, so it can't be too complex or necessarily require laboratory equipment. The taste, goodness and colour of the ingredient(s) – whatever fruit, flower or root or combination you choose – is first extracted. Roots require boiling but, with the others, it is merely a case of crushing and soaking in water which, for convenience, is usually quite hot. The ratio of water to fruit, etc., is generally a gallon (4½ litres) to 3 or 4 lbs (1½ – 2 kg). (If you are using dried fruit, the ratio will be about 1 gallon to 1 lb.) Apples and plums, if well crushed, require much less. The resulting mixture is called *must* and it is left to soak for a short number of days, depending on the ingredient used. We often use an ordinary lidless polythene bucket for this, covered with a cloth to keep flies and dust out, but a bin or bowl is better as a piece of board may be then laid over the cloth as a further safeguard. Stir and squeeze out the juice every day – the Continentals traditionally do this by having the girls stomp round it in their bare feet, so we're sure you won't mind using your hands. The mixture, when ready, is strained – through a fine non-metal sieve or a jelly bag.

Stage Two: Fermentation

Stage two involves the fermentation of this liquid. Basically, the must – or more correctly its fruit-sugar and the sugar you've added to it – is 'fed' to yeast which reduces it to carbon dioxide and alcohol. The carbon dioxide bubbles up to the surface and is dispensed; the alcohol – thank Providence – remains. Chemically, this is a most complex happening; in practice, it is an age-old and straightforward example of white magic.

You add sugar, usually the same weight as that of the original amount of fruit; in earlier times honey was used. It is usual to add 3 lbs (1½ kg) sugar per gallon (4½ litres) of strained liquid or an equal weight to that of the fruit originally. If only half this amount is used, the yeast will use it all up and the wine will be very dry; if more than 4 lb (2 kg) per gallon (4½ litres) is used the action of the yeast will be inhibited by the alcohol produced, so that the result will be a sweet wine. Only by experience (and keeping records from year to year) will you know exactly what you want. Demerara sugar always adds to the flavour but plain white sugar does fine.

This is the usual time also to add any other ingredients (except isinglass or any other fining or clearing agent), i.e. raisins, ginger, lemons, tannin, nutrients etc. and, of course, yeast.

Some winemakers like to use raisins to give their wines 'body', which they feel might otherwise be lacking, and as an aid to fermentation. The usual amount is ¼ lb per gallon (125 g to 4½ litres) of strained liquid. We usually try to do without any raisins at all for they tend to interfere with the more delicate flavours of the wild fruits. Experience alone will tell you how much you personally prefer to do with.

Nutrient is nitrogenous matter which feeds the yeast and thus aids fermentation. Some country wines, particularly those made from flowers, are likely to be deficient in the foods the yeast requires, so it is always a good idea to add nutrient. Moreover, the extra nutrient is a great help if we want strong dry wine. Vitamin B is especially to be recommended. Any good winemaking book will tell you how to make up your own nutrients but we rely on proprietary brands such as Benerva which may be obtained from your local chemist.

We normally use them at the following rates per gallon (4½ litres):

Fruit wine	1 (3 milligram) tablet
Plant and root wines	2 (3 milligram) tablets
Flower wines	3 (3 milligram) tablets

We occasionally advocate the use of a pectin-destroying agent in some of the wine recipes; many winemakers make a habit of using such an agent with all their fruit wines but we think this unnecessary. Pectins – which are aggravated by boiling when making the must – may cause the wine to be unclear. Proprietary brands of pectin-destroying enzymes may be obtained from chemists or from home-winemakers' suppliers and should be added to the cooled pulp or juice of the fruit at the rate recommended by the manufacturers.

Citric acid may be required to help in fermentation. We use lemons; rarely more than one to the gallon of must; often many fruits are already so acidic as not to require any addition. Sufficient tannin is possessed by most fruits; yet some winemakers make it a practice to add a tablespoon or two of cold strong tea.

Yeast is the ingredient which brings about fermentation (by acting on the sugar to convert it into alcohol). Any article or book on winemaking which we have ever read has had so much to say about yeasts that we suspect the beginner's nerve often fails at this point. Let us say with our hands on our hearts that we have used yeast in whatever shape or form that came readily to hand and never with bad results. Most often this has been the dried brewer's yeast tablets or powder sold by chemists as a tonic or health food. Ordinary baker's yeast, the sort sold for home-made bread, will do quite well. When you feel you are something of an expert then wild horses will not be able to hold you back from using the specially prepared wine yeasts and starter bottles. Normally 1 tspn of yeast is added to each gallon (4½ litres) of must.

We would advise two stages in fermentation. If we are going to strain again – and this ought to be done anywhere between four and ten days later – we do the initial fermentation in the same bucket as was used to contain the must. The yeast is added when the liquid is lukewarm, not over 70°F (21°C), and it must be left where it will remain lukewarm, so as to keep the fermentation going. It is a good idea, at this point, to add an ordinary fruit preserving tablet (Campden tablets supply the necessary sulphur dioxide in convenient form) to sterilize the must; we dislike using more than 1 tablet per gallon (4½ litres). Give the mixture a good stirring every day. The vessel should be kept well covered (gases must be allowed to escape, of course!) because wine in the making must be protected from air as much as possible. Wine ought to ferment anaerobically (without air) and if left too long in the bucket in contact with air the flavour will spoil; usually 4 or 5 days is enough. (Many beginners who do not know this may get the bitter, undrinkable wine which results; this fault may also occur later on if bottles, etc. are not topped up to just below the cork.)

Strain for the second time. Then it's into the fermentation jar and bung down with a cork containing the fermentation lock. Leave where the liquid is warm enough to encourage fermentation, a process which will last for many weeks. Again, the books will go into great detail about fermentation locks and bungs and God alone knows what. If you have these pieces of equipment, well and good. If you haven't, you can stuff the tops of bottles or cover jars with cotton wool and still make good wine. The fermentation lock or cotton wool enables the gas to escape from the fermenting liquid and prevents harmful elements entering and destroying your wine.

How do you know your wine is fermenting? If you have a fermentation lock fitted, you cannot fail to notice the gas bubbling; otherwise you will have to listen. Put your ear to the mouth of the container and you'll hear the activity if fermentation is taking place, a sort of 'crackle in a whisper', as a child once described it to us. At any rate, the slight hissing sound is unmistakable when you hear it. If the fermentation is strong, you will notice bubbles rising to the surface.

The fermentation part of the business may take a couple of months or more. With experience, you will know when to add extra sugar to keep fermentation going. If your wine has been made in autumn, it will ferment into the new calendar months only if warmth is given to it. (Friends of ours always ferment their wine in the hot-press.) If the temperature is not kept up to the usual 65°F (18°C) or thereabouts, the fermentation will cease before the maximum alcohol has been produced. The unwary novice, believing the process is then complete, may bung down his barrel and put it away or (worse still) bottle and be dismayed to find on the new warmth of spring that his bungs and corks have blown out or bottles burst. Bottles with screw-on lids are potentially dangerous unless fermentation has been absolutely completed. (Any time we were forced to fall back on them, we stored them in cardboard containers which were originally packaging for soft drinks.)

If corks, etc., 'blow', the wine will be exposed to bacteria; one common type converts the alcohol to vinegar. Oxidisation, with its resulting bad taste, might also occur, or moulds grow from airborne spores. (Bottling with imperfect stoppers can, of course, produce the same undesirable results.) Prevention, in the form of completed fermentation, is absolutely necessary.

Stage Three: Clearing and Maturing

The fermentation lock really comes into its own when you wish to know if fermentation is finished, as no more gas bubbles will be passing through the lock. Otherwise, you must listen very intently and look very carefully to make sure that all activity has ceased in your container. When fermentation is absolutely finished, it is time to draw off the wine, leaving the sediment at the bottom of the container. If you have made your wine in a barrel with a tap, you will have no trouble in drawing it off. Otherwise, you must syphon it off. Again, you will find several different types of syphon – some comparatively expensive – on offer from the shops, but a length of cheap rubber tubing from your chemist, even if not quite as handy, will do the trick just as well. Be warned, however: if the internal diameter of the tube is too great, it will tend to suck up the sediment. We find ¼ inch (6 mm) internal diameter handiest. In actual fact, experienced winemakers may syphon off or rack twice before fermentation is absolutely finished. The first time is normally after two to three months when the cloudy wine begins to clear from the top down and a thick layer of yeast and solids sinks to the bottom. They then continue fermentation and rack again when the wine is completely clear.

You may care to bottle at this point but as a general rule the longer the wine is kept in bulk the better. Therefore, it is more usual to wash the sediment out of the container and return your wine to it. Make sure to fill it right up, even if this means 'topping up' with a little wine, brandy or even water. Put in a cool place. Listen 'in' after a couple of days to make doubly sure fermentation has stopped. Leave the wine to clear and mature for some six months or so – at least you should, but at first you won't if you are human. This is why we like to have more than one container – we may then succumb to temptation with the one and leave the others undefiled.

After syphoning or tapping, you may add isinglass if a clearing agent is required. Always give your wine a chance to clear naturally, even if this takes over six months. When necessary, dissolve the isinglass in a few spoonfuls of hot water, mix well by shaking in a little of the wine and add to your container, mixing it in well. In many cases all that is needed for the wine to clear is that it be moved to a much lower temperature when fermentation is over.

Stage Four: Bottling

Whatever kind of bottles you use, make sure they have been well washed in very hot water. Be scrupulous as regards cleanliness. Tap your barrel (first having removed the bung on top) or syphon off; this is where the glass containers really prove their worth as you can keep a wary eye on the sediment. Fill your bottles to about half-way up the neck. Wine bottles and corks may be bought. The better-type corks are those with a head or stopper. It is a good idea to leave them overnight in water to soften them but a few minutes in boiling water will do for sterilizing. There are quite cheap tools available for corking and there is the housewife's way, holding the bottle in one hand (a tea cloth will aid gripping) and hammering in the cork with a flat and reasonably stout piece of wood. The corks will shrivel in time if the bottle is not laid on its side so that the wine itself keeps them swollen.

* * * * *

Of course this is not the only way of making wine and, as you gain experience, you will find the way which suits you best. Normally, the amounts of ingredients as specified in recipes will not necessarily have to be adapted for the different methods. On the other hand, however, the experienced winemaker will adapt recipes to suit his or her own taste. Recipes are never any more than useful guides and it is good that the beginner recognises this from the onset.

WEIGHTS AND MEASURES

We have given both avoirdupois and metric measures for ingredients in the recipes. Converting one to another is an awkward business and therefore we have given the most convenient equivalents when measures need not be absolutely accurate, rounding off amounts by addition or subtraction as best suited the recipes. This accounts for any seeming discrepancies in conversion.

Our winemaking has become more and more simple – and 'pure' – over the years. Since this book was first published we have tended to shun all fruit preserving tablets and even pectin-destroying agents (but, then, it never worries us in the slightest if our wine is occasionally less than crystal clear).

part four

THE WILD FOOD & RECIPES

BEECH

Fagus sylvatica

A tall, often over 100 ft (30 m), stately, shade-giving tree with distinctive soft, bright green leaves, which, withered and brown, tend to remain on the tree throughout the winter. Our picture shows the autumn husks; the one at bottom right has opened its four lobes, uncovering the brown nuts, four in number and three-sided, which may be eaten raw or roasted and salted.

This common, fine tree surely needs little description. Tall and stately when full-grown, the epithet *bile* is given to it in Irish Gaelic, indicating a tree of distinction: *fáidhbhile.* It has a rather smooth, grey-coloured bark but is best recognised, perhaps, by its leaves which are bright green in colour, shiny, small for a tree of its size, delicate, oval, indented. The leaves may be used as a salad and the nuts (called mast, beechmast or buckmast) were much used in olden times, especially as pig-food. A fine vegetable oil may be extracted from the mast as well – quite a large amount of this is made in Germany to this day. A couple of hundred years ago, butter was made commercially from the extract in Britain. The liqueur made from its leaves was a localised drink in England.

BEECH LEAF LIQUEUR

Although this recipe came to us from England, it is most probably French in origin. Gather the leaves in April and cram into a pint (½ litre) glass jar or earthenware crock until three-quarters full or more; fill with gin until the leaves are covered. Cover and leave for two weeks before straining. Dissolve a half pound (250 g) of sugar (better still, if you like your liqueurs quite syrupy, genuine honey) in as little hot water as it takes to do so and add to the gin. Mix and bottle when cold.

BLACKBERRY

Rubis fruiticosus

This most common of shrubs grows in tangled disarray often up to 7 ft (2 m) or more in height. The strong shoot at the left has five leaflets on its stalk; the second-year shoot, three-leafleted and bearing the fruit, is on the right. The serrated leaflets are whitish underneath and in autumn will have turned to wonderful reds and purples. The berries (green and red and hard when unripe) are made up of luscious drupelets or grains, and are a shiny, purple-black. Is there any need to add that it is a most prickly shrub?

The bramble (in Irish Gaelic *dris* or *drisleog* which merely seems to indicate a 'thorny bush,' for the same term is applied to the wild rose bushes) is the most common fruit-bearing bush in our hedges; and so it never occurred to us to describe it until, in the course of a survey conducted in a city school, it was discovered that an appallingly large percentage of city children apparently did not know of its existence. Really, we should not have been surprised: an equally large percentage thought milk was produced in factories! On the other hand, even those who could recognise a blackberry (or 'bramble berry') were, on the whole, unconvinced of its value. We cannot resist, therefore, quoting T. W. Sanders in his *Fruit and its Cultivation*, published well over a half century ago: 'Everyone knows how fruitful these plants are in their wild state... good as they are, it is not worth while attempting their culture in gardens when fruit can be so plentifully obtained in a wild state.'

A generation ago, blackberry picking time was an event on the calendar almost as significant as that of Christmas or Easter. Entire families from town and city, armed with buckets and 'tilly' cans, descended like invading armies on the countryside and plundered the roadsides, hedges, woods and waste-ground; few enough were the houses without blackberry jam or jelly (full of Vitamin C) during the winter months. There must be many, many people who cherish happy childhood memories of such family adventures, yet have overlooked in the rush of modern living to pass on the same to their own children.

For those who have not yet had the pleasure of meeting the blackberry (thorns and all!), we will attempt to describe this lowly but very worthy bush. Certainly, those who have ever fallen into one or laddered a nylon in one, will hardly need reminding that it is a very prickly shrub, usually growing in straggly clumps in every hedgerow. Even the leaves are rough and indented; the leaflets stand either three or five on a stalk and turn a purply brown in the autumn. All summer and, to a lesser extent, in early autumn, their myriads of flowers, pure white or tinged with purple, against their dark foliage remind one of the stars in the harvest night-sky. From August onwards, the fruit, in large clusters, turns from green to red to a luscious black purple. This colour-change gives rise to the story of the American visitor to Ireland who exclaimed, 'why do you call them blackberries when they're red?' and was non-plussed by the answer, 'sure they're only red when they're green!'

In Irish Gaelic, the same anomaly occurs. *Sméara,* which indicates something blurred and red such as embers, is applied to the berries – until they are ripe, when they become *sméara dubha* or 'black (red) berries'. Indeed, when the berries are at their deepest colour and are most luscious, the Irish-speaker calls them *sméara ciaráin,* in translation, something like 'jet-black red-berries'. Both Gaelic *dris* (the Scots also use *droighean*) and Anglo-Saxon *bramble* refer to the thorns and briars. The Welsh name is *miar.*

The berry will remain long after early October, but folk tradition is all against picking them at this period. The big horse fairs used to be held in the latter end of September and, when we were young, we were warned never to eat blackberries 'after Ballyboggin Fair' or 'after the Fair of Ballinasloe' and so on. The old folk believed 'the maggot' came into them then and, even if they remained uncontaminated, by mid-October blackberries may be musty, mildewed or tasteless. The fruit is composed of small grains (like a black raspberry, but round in shape) and is at its best during the summer and early autumn for eating raw with the addition of cream or plain milk, and sugar. The less juicy fruit farther back the stalk is excellent for jams, jellies, tarts and wines, and will remain plentiful until early October.

BLACKBERRY FOOL *Serves 2–3*

½ lb (225 g) blackberries
2 tspn. vanilla essence
Sugar to taste
Cream

Place the fruit in a pan with enough water to cover it. Cover the saucepan and cook slowly until berries are soft. Add sugar to taste and the vanilla essence. Stir until sugar is melted. Put through a sieve. Whip cream and fold into the blackberries. Unless you have a very sweet tooth, be careful not to add the sugar with too heavy a hand.

BLACKBERRY AND ELDERBERRY CHUTNEY

1 lb (500 g) blackberries
1 lb (500 g) elderberries
1 large onion
¼ lb (100 g) chopped raisins
2 lb (1 kg) crab apples
1 pint (½ litre) of malt vinegar
4 oz (100 g) brown sugar
Salt to taste
Assorted spices: ½ tspn. approx. ground ginger, cinnamon, nutmeg, mustard, cayenne pepper, ground cloves.

Prepare the fruit and put them in a saucepan with the vinegar and mash them well. Chop the onion and add with the raisins to the mixture in the saucepan together with the spices and sugar. Simmer all together about fifteen minutes until thick, stirring all the time. Pour into heated bottles and cap well.

BLACKBERRY AND APPLE MOUSSE *Serves 6-8*

1 lb (500 g) blackberries
1 lb (500 g) crabs (or cooking apples)
4 oz (100 g) castor sugar
1 good tbspn. gelatine
Juice of 1 lemon
2 whites of egg
½ cup of water

Sprinkle gelatine on the strained lemon juice and leave to one side. Put prepared blackberries and apples, peeled, cored and sliced, with the water in a saucepan. Mix in 3 oz (75 g) of the sugar, cover with a lid and simmer until the fruit is tender, about ¼ hour. Remove saucepan from cooker and thoroughly stir in gelatine and lemon juice. The mixture must be put through a sieve, then left until cold and beginning to thicken. At this point whisk whites of egg until stiff and then beat in the remaining 1 oz (25 g) sugar. Fold into the fruit and leave in the fridge to become firm.

BLACKBERRY AND APPLE SWEET *Serves 4-6*

4 – 6 apples
1 lb (500 g) blackberries
Honey or sugar to taste

Wash, peel and core the apples. Mash the blackberries to a pulp and add sugar or honey. Stuff the cored apples with the blackberry mixture. Put in a fireproof dish and add enough water to prevent fruit from burning. Cover and put in a moderate oven until apples are cooked. Serve with cream.

BLACKBERRY PIE *Serves 4-6*

6 oz (150 g) flour
3 oz (75 g) margerine or shortening
1 apple
3 – 4 oz (75 – 100 g) sugar
½ tspn. cinnamon (optional)
2 or 3 cups blackberries

Mix the shortening into the flour until crumbly. Sprinkle with water and mix with a fork until all the flour is moistened. Make the dough into a ball and roll out so as to line a greased sandwich tin. Keep trimmings and a few strips for the top for decoration. Cook the blackberries, sugar and cinnamon lightly in just enough water to keep them from burning. If the filling is a little too watery, thicken strained juice with cornflour and pour over fruit. Add to pastry. Slice the apple into small pieces and place these and strips of pastry on top of the filling. Put into oven 450°F (230°C) Reg. 8 and bake until golden brown, 30–40 minutes.

BLACKBERRY AND CRAB APPLE PUDDING *Serves 6-8*

1 small loaf of bread
8 oz (225 g) sugar
½ lb (225 g) crab apples (if ripe enough) or cooking apples
1 lb (500 g) blackberries
Water

This pudding should be made the day before it is needed. Remove the crusts from the thickly sliced loaf (stale bread is best). Line the sides and bottom of a deep pudding bowl with the slices overlapping. Simmer the blackberries and crabs (peeled and sliced), in about ½ pint (¼ litre) water for a few minutes. Drain off the water and add the sugar to the fruit (remember crabs can be very sour). Fill the bowl with the mixture and put a layer of moistened bread over it. Cover with greaseproof paper and put a weight on top and leave in the fridge overnight. Serve with cream.

BLACKBERRY SYRUP *(1)*

Put the fruit in a large jar – Kilner jars are very suitable – and stand, covered, in a saucepan of boiling water and cook until all the juice is extracted. Strain through a jelly bag (overnight), measure juice and weigh out the sugar at the rate of 1 lb (500 g) per pint (½ litre) of juice. Warm the sugar. Meanwhile, boil the juice gently for ten minutes. Remove from heat and add the sugar, stirring until dissolved. Bring to the boil and boil rapidly for five minutes. Skim, bottle and sterilize as advised in the section on bottling. This gives a thick syrup which can be diluted with water or soda water to make a refreshing drink; for a night cap, excellent for colds, add whiskey and water and serve very hot.

BLACKBERRY SYRUP *(2)*

4 – 6 lb (2 – 3 kg) blackberries
6 oz (150 g) sugar per pint (½ litre) of juice

Bring to the boil and then simmer blackberries in a pint (½ litre) of water for forty-five minutes. Strain through a jelly bag (overnight). Measure juice and weigh out the sugar as above. Boil the juice gently for ten minutes. Remove from heat and add the warmed sugar stirring until it is dissolved. Return saucepan to heat and boil gently for twenty minutes. Skim, bottle and sterilize as advised in the section on bottling. The above measurements will give about a quart (1 litre) of syrup.

BLACKBERRY JAM (WITH APPLE JUICE)

4 lb (2 kg) blackberries
4 lb (2 kg) sugar
1 lb (500 g) apples to provide juice
Juice of 1 lemon

Prepare the apple juice by boiling to a pulp 1 lb (500 g) apples in ½ pint (¼ litre) water, and straining. Add ¼ pint (150 ml) water and lemon juice to the blackberries and simmer until tender. Add sugar and apple juice. Boil, stirring constantly, until it sets when tested. Skim and proceed as advised in the section on jam-making.

BLACKBERRY AND CRAB APPLE JAM

2 lb (1 kg) blackberries
2 lb (1 kg) crab apples (or green apples)
4 lb (2 kg) sugar
Grated rind of lemon

Peel and core the crabs and simmer to a pulp in a ½ pint (¼ litre) water. Add the grated rind of the lemon. Now simmer blackberries in a ¼ pint (150 ml) water. Combine and add 4 lb (2 kg) sugar and bring to the boil, stirring constantly until the sugar is melted. Boil rapidly until jam sets when tested. Skim and proceed as advised in the section on jam-making.

BLACKBERRY AND CULTIVATED APPLE JAM

2 lb (1 kg) blackberries
1 lb (500 g) apples
Sugar

The apples must be peeled and cored before being cut up and boiled in a little water until they become soft. Sieve, and put along with the blackberries in the saucepan. Weigh and add an equal weight of warmed sugar. Bring to the boil slowly and stir continuously until the sugar has dissolved. Then, boil rapidly until jam sets when tested, about twenty to twenty-five minutes. Skim and proceed as advised in the section on jam-making.

BLACKBERRY AND ELDERBERRY JAM

See under Elderberry and Blackberry Jam (page 102).

BLACKBERRY AND ROSEHIP JAM

3 lb (1½ kg) blackberries
6 oz (150 g) rosehips
Sugar
Water

It is absolutely necessary to cut the hips open with a sharp knife and take out all the seed and pith, as the seeds can cause bowel irritation, being covered with sharp hairs; only the flesh, chopped up as fine as reasonably possible, is used. To soften them, put them for twenty-four hours in just enough water to cover them, or simmer gently for two hours. Put through a sieve and add to the prepared blackberries, which also have been simmered in a very little water until tender. Empty the fruit juice into a saucepan and for each pint (½ litre) add 1 lb (500 g) warmed sugar. Stir until the sugar is dissolved. Boil quickly until jam sets when tested. Skim and proceed as advised in the section on jam-making.

BLACKBERRY AND CRAB APPLE JELLY

See under Crab Apple and Blackberry Jelly (page 85).

BLACKBERRY AND APPLE MARMALADE

Blackberries
Apples
Sugar
Cider and water

Equal weights of apples and blackberries are used. Slice the apples but do not peel or core, and put them and the blackberries into the saucepan and add just enough cider and water (half and half) to allow the mixture to be simmered for an hour, stirring continuously as there is a danger of burning. Put the pulp through a sieve, measure and add 1 lb (500 g) warmed sugar for each pint (½ litre) of pulp. Bring slowly to the boil (still stirring continuously) and simmer until it 'sheets' when poured from the side of the spoon in the manner described in the recipe for Plum Butter (page 139). Pot and seal while still hot. This makes a very thick and palatable marmalade.

BLACKBERRY JELLY

4 lb (2 kg) blackberries
Sugar
Juice of lemon or ½ tspn. citric or tartaric acid
¾ pint (450 ml) water

If some unripe berries are included this will give a nice sharpness to the flavour. Simmer fruit and lemon juice in ¾ pint (450 ml) water until fruit is tender. Strain overnight through a jelly bag. Measure the juice and to each pint (½ litre) add 1 lb (500 g) warmed sugar. Bring to boiling point and boil quickly until mixture sets when tested. Skim and proceed as advised in section on jelly making.

To spice: add 4 cloves and ½ stick cinnamon to the fruit. To each pint (½ litre) of juice, include 1 tablespoonful of vinegar when you are adding the sugar.

BLACKBERRY AND CULTIVATED APPLE JELLY

1 lb (500 g) blackberries
3 lb (1½ kg) apples
Sugar
Lemon juice to taste

Do not peel or core apples but cut into quarters or smaller pieces and put into saucepan. Spice if desired with cinnamon or cloves. Bruise the blackberries, cover with water to level of fruit, simmer until pulpy. Strain overnight, measure juice and add 1 lb (500 g) sugar for every pint (½ litre) of juice. Stir and heat slowly until sugar dissolves, then boil and cook rapidly for some 40 minutes or until jelly sets when tested. Skim and proceed as advised in section on jelly making.

BLACKBERRY AND ROWANBERRY JELLY

Blackberries
Rowanberries
Sugar

First prepare rowanberries, putting them into a saucepan with just enough water to cover them. Boil, stirring occasionally, for thirty minutes by which time all fruit (if properly ripe) should have burst. Strain.

Weigh blackberries, put into a saucepan adding a small cupful of water to each 1 lb (500 g) of blackberries. Boil for twenty minutes, then strain.

Pour equal quantities of the two juices into the preserving pan (any left-over juice may be used for some other recipe) and to each pint (½ litre) of juice add 1 lb (500 g) of warmed sugar. Dissolve and boil for 30 minutes, stirring occasionally until it sets when tested. Proceed as advised in section on jelly making. Some palates may find this jelly very tart.

MIXUM-GATHERUM JELLY

A combination of crabs, blackberries and rosehips

1 lb (500 g) blackberries
Sugar
1 lb (500 g) rosehips
2 lb (1 kg) crabs
Water or cider

If other fruits are added (for instance, damsons or bullaces, or both), it is probably best to use equal amounts by weight of the fruits. Add enough water or cider to almost cover fruit. Simmer until pulpy. Strain, taking great care as always when rose hips are used to prevent fibres from getting into the juice (see page 42). To each pint (½ litre) of juice, add 1 1b (500 g) sugar. When sugar is dissolved, boil rapidly until jelly sets when tested (about thirty minutes). Skim and proceed as advised in the section on jelly making.

BLACKBERRY LIQUEUR

1 lb (500 g) blackberries
1 tbspn. brandy or ½ glass whiskey
1 lb (500 g) sugar
1 tbspn. water

This hardly merits the title of 'liqueur' but it might just be ideal for making the afternoon of a party. Put the fruit, sugar and water in a covered jar, stand in a saucepan of boiling water and simmer for a couple of hours. Strain and boil the juice for a further quarter of an hour or so and skim if necessary. When cool, mix in the spirits and bottle.

BLACKBERRY DRINK

Much loved by campers, we give this as we ourselves have made it by the camp fire. Simply cram ripe berries into a billycan until it is half full and top up with water. Bring to the boil and then simmer for a while, stirring occasionally, add sugar to taste and a couple of squares of chocolate if handy. Strain. Served hot, it makes an excellent bedtime drink; if bottled cold, it makes a most refreshing drink when cycling or hiking.

BLACKBERRY WINE *(1)*

5 lb (2½ kg) blackberries
1 gallon (4½ litres) boiling water
1 tspn. yeast
2½ lb (1¼ kg) white sugar

This is a very simple recipe which we have found makes an excellent dry wine. Make sure your fruit is clean and pour boiling water on the fruit and bruise with a wooden spoon. Leave for three days, stirring at intervals and squeezing the fruit daily. Strain, add yeast and sugar and keep fermentation going by adding a little more sugar. Syphon and leave to mature for six months before bottling. Leave for a year or so if possible. If you prefer a very sweet wine, you could use up to 4 lb (2 kg) sugar.

BLACKBERRY WINE *(2)*

4 lb (2 kg) blackberries
6 oz (150 g) raisins
2½ lb (1¼ kg) sugar
6 pints (3½ litres) boiling water
1 tspn. yeast
Campden tablet
Nutrient
Pectin-destroying agent

Bruise the berries and chop the raisins, mix and pour on the boiling water, cool, add Campden tablet and pectin-destroying agent. You may proceed then as in the previous recipe. However, if you wish for a more sophisticated wine, add in the nutrient, yeast and a pound (500 g) of the sugar and ferment on the pulp until the third day; don't forget to squeeze twice a day. Strain, stir in a further 1½ lb (700 g) sugar and continue fermentation as usual. Add the remaining 1 lb (500 g) sugar from time to time in 3–4 oz (75–100 g) lots and as the fermentation slows down. Proceed as with previous recipe.

BLACKTHORN

Prunus spinosa

A dense shrub, normally from 8 ft (2½ m) to 10 ft (3 m) high with long spines and darkish green, oval leaves. The bark is a distinctive, rich black-brown. The sloe is small, round, dark-blue and often covered with a whitish bloom.

Bliain na n-áirní, bliain bhrónach;
Bliain na sgeachóirí, bliain bhreágh.

A sloe year is a low year:
A haw year is a braw year.

So bitter is it, one bite of a sloe is just about enough to convince anybody that the fruit of the blackthorn could not possibly bear any resemblance to the Victoria plum or some such luscious domesticated variety. In fact, incredible though it may seem, it is generally accepted that the sloe is an ancestor of all cultivated and wild plums. Not only that but it would seem that man has been using it for food for thousands of years. Don't let its acid taste when raw deter you from making it into a good sharp jelly with a rich claret colour (lovely with meat or on scones), an excellent port-like wine and a superb gin-liqueur. In fact, sloe makes such good wine that, according to Brook two hundred years ago, it was much used 'by fraudulent Wine Merchants in adulterating port wine, for which purpose it is well adapted on account of its astringency, slight acidity, and deep red colour.' He goes on to add that 'many a fop when taking his '*poort wind*' and tapping his boots with his beautiful blackthorn stick, is little aware that both '*wind*' and stick have the *same origin.* It has been stated that there is more port wine (so called) drunk in England alone, than is manufactured in Portugal!'

The sloe, called *áirne* in Gaelic, was always much prized in Ireland, as the numerous references to it in early and later poetry suggest. Researches at Holy Cross Abbey showed that the medieval monks were partial to it in the form of an alcoholic drink akin to gin, and famed Killarney, *Cill Áirne,* 'the Church of the sloe-bushes,' is only one of many places called after the berry. Welsh *eirin* for the sloe is cognate with the Irish name and both Gaelic *draighean dubh* and Welsh *draen ddu* mean, simply, 'black thorn.' The more usual Scots Gaelic name is *buileastair* (from old French *béloce*, a bullace) and so the tree and its fruit are often called 'bullisters' in Scotland and in the north of Ireland.

The juice of the berries was used for medicinal purposes: 'it is a rough purge', states an old book, 'but a good one'. It was also used to dye linen a light-blue. The much-maligned Irish cudgel was often cut from the blackthorn (*Draighean Dubh* or *Crann Áirne*). The leaves were made into a rather astringent tea ('Irish Tea') and also into a tobacco. It is a very common bush, especially in hedgerows, all over these islands (though less so in the more northerly areas). It grows normally from about 8 to 12 ft (2½–3 m) high, has a dark bark and darkish-green, oval leaves; one of its most noticeable features is its long and very sharp thorns. It is the first native bush of all to flower, doing so in April even before it itself becomes leafed; and its clusters of little white or green-white flowers make almost as fine a showing as those of the hawthorn which arrays itself soon after. The small, round, blue-black sour plums may seem ripe in September but should not be picked until after the first hard frost which makes their tough skins more porous. As with all plums, the sloe contains a stone and its skin is covered with a dust or 'bloom' which is natural yeast.

SLOE JELLY

Sloe for all its acidity makes an excellent jelly. However, used by itself, it is probably too tart for most modern tastes. We, therefore, recommend that it be combined with crab apple, and this recipe is given under Crab Apple and Sloe Jelly (page 86).

SLOE WINE *(1)*

1 gallon (4½ litres) sloes
1 gallon (4½ litres) boiling water
3 – 4 lb (1½ – 2 kg) sugar
1 tspn. yeast

This is a recipe from West Cork, which a friend of ours gave us on request after we had found her wine to be an excellent sweet 'port'. Pour boiling water over the sloes, mash and cover and leave for a week, stirring every day. Strain. Heat some of the must, add the sugar to it and stir to dissolve. Add this to the rest of the liquid. When cooled to about 70°F (21°C) or less, add the yeast and place in a warm place to ferment. Leave in the cask to ripen for a month or so, when the wine should be tasted and more sugar added if it should be too bitter. The fermentation lock should be refitted and the wine left to clear in a cooler place for a further month or so. It should be matured for a year or more. Isinglass may have to be used to clear the wine.

SLOE WINE *(2)*

3 lb (1½ kg) sloes
3 – 3½ lb (1½ – 1¾ kg) sugar
8 oz (250 g) raisins
1 gallon (4½ litres) boiling water
Pectin-destroying enzyme
1 tspn. yeast

If you dislike using raisins, you could increase the weight of both sloes and sugar. Pour the boiling water on the sloes, mash, add the chopped raisins and steep for two to four days before straining. Dissolve the sugar in a little of the must by warming and stirring, return to the container and, when cool, add the yeast (and a nutrient, especially if no raisins are used). Keep fermentation going as long as possible by adding more sugar, then rack and bottle. 1 oz (25 g) isinglass may be necessary to clear the wine.

If you wish to ferment on the pulp, do so for ten days before straining into the fermenting jar. After a month, test for bitterness, add sugar if necessary, and keep fermenting at a slower pace (i.e. at a cooler temperature) for another month or so. Sloe wine, in common with most other wines, should be matured for about a year.

SLOE GIN

When we were children, it was quite common for people, especially the younger ones, to cram a bottle with sugar and sloes (previously pricked with a pin), cover with lukewarm water, cap or cork securely and bury it until Christmas. This was called Sloe Gin and was probably mildly alcoholic because of the action of the wild yeasts.

What is nowadays called Sloe Gin is really a Gin Liqueur. Most experts would recommend wiping the sloes or washing them to get rid of wild yeasts. Whether the berries have been exposed to frost or not, prick them with a darning needle. Half fill a jar (Kilner jars are ideal for this purpose) with sloes and add about the same weight of sugar as of fruit. Castor sugar is to be recommended as it dissolves easier. Fill up to the top with gin and cap tightly. By this stage, you may have cared to add a few drops of almond essence; otherwise, it is a good idea to add a few skinned almonds after a couple of weeks. It may be difficult getting your sugar to dissolve, even by vigorous shaking; try turning the jars upside down every day or so. Leave in a reasonably warm place for two to three months; if you are a normal homebrewer, Christmas will determine the length of time! Some like to strain well (through thick flannel or doubled muslin) but others like to eat the fruit while drinking the gin! They say it even gets better if matured longer; we wouldn't know...

CARRAGEEN MOSS / SEA MOSS

Chondrus crispus

Flat-stalked with dark purple-brown fronds (which sometimes may seem in the water to tend towards its off-white colour when bleached). Carrageen has a characteristic fan-shape but may appear more like the lower drawing as current or tide moves it.

Mná i locháin
In íochtar diaidh-thrá,
A gcótaí craptha,
Scáilí thíos fúthu:
Támh-radharc síothach
San Earrach thiar.

Women in rock-pools at the low tide's edge, their petticoats bundled up, reflections under them: a peaceable, trance-like scene of a western Spring.
Máirtín Ó Direáin (ó An Earrach Thiar)

Although very much associated with Ireland, even to the extent of being known as Irish Moss, this seaweed grows plentifully along the south-westerly Atlantic shores of Britain and Europe. Indeed, much 'Irish' moss has been collected for commercial purposes from the southern shores of the United Kingdom. It is also known in Britain as Sea Moss and Carragheen; the Gaelic is *Carraigín,* a diminutive of *carraig,* a rock. Sea moss is used a good deal commercially – as a health food and also in the manufacture of soups, jellies and ice-creams. It is found on rocks and stones on middle and lower shores, is usually a dark purple-brown colour and evolves from a narrow stem into clusters of fronds, which tend to be fan-shaped and tongued. As the verse above suggests, it should be harvested at low tide in late-spring and early summer. As with all seaweed, it should be washed well and, if not to be dried, eaten as soon as possible. The weed should be bleached in the drying. Lay the fronds on the grass where it will get the rain (otherwise, it will need plenty of sprinkling with fresh water). After a week or so, it will have turned to a creamy-white colour, when it must be kept dry and exposed to sunlight until thoroughly dried.

The making of blancmange or mould from carrageen moss is simple. Take about a ¼ oz (6 g) or half-cup weed to a pint (½ litre) of milk. First, steep the dried moss in cold water for about fifteen minutes, drain and trim off any of the root or dark discoloured parts. Simmer in the milk for a half hour or until the mixture is thick enough to coat the back of a wooden spoon. Stir in a dessert-spoon of sugar and serve hot, perhaps with stewed fruit, or pour into a wetted mould and leave in a cool place to set. Either way, milk or cream go well with the dish. We have found carrageen to be something of an acquired taste and many people would like additional flavouring, such as chopped ginger, grated lemon rind or vanilla, which is added when the mixture is to be simmered. A pinch or two of salt is also recommended and 'sweet teeth' may call for more sugar. A jelly is made in the same way, using water instead of milk and with the addition of a beaten egg or egg-white just before the mixture is ready to be poured.

You may like to be imaginative and use carrageen moss in other desserts, in a soufflé or pudding or flan, for instance; in all cases, the basic simmering must be carried out but there is no reason why more milk may not be used if required.

COWSLIP AND PRIMROSE

Primula veris and Primula vulgaris

Primrose (below): A small, vigorous-looking plant of hedgerows and shady banks, with appealing, pale yellow, five-petalled flowers, one to each stalk. The crinkly leaves grow in rosette, low to the ground and have downy undersides. The stout stem is well hidden.

Cowslip (left): The different kinds of cowslip all look similar, with umbels of strong yellow, orange-spotted flowers wobbling on long stalks up to 8 inches (20 cm) or so in height. The wrinkled leaves and slightly downy underneath remain more or less at ground level and grow from the base of the stem. It prefers open, grassy spaces.

'Where is the Man,' enthused the wonderful Richard Brook in his *Family Herbal* nearly two hundred years ago, 'who has not felt the heart-thrilling sensation, the delightful emotions not to be described at first beholding the Cowslip and Primrose, these lovely harbingers of Spring?' This is still true, except that the emotion today may be mixed with a heart-chilling sensation if it is recalled that there are prophecies from naturalists in Britain that in some areas the plants could be in danger in the not too distant future. The plants are closely related, as the Latin names indicate: *Primula veris* (Cowslip) and *Primula vulgaris*; the Irish Gaelic also indicates the same: *Bainne Bó Bainne* (Cowslip) and *Bainne Bó Bleacht,* both meaning something like 'the Milk of the Milch Cows,' i.e. that it is these (or the grass at the period of their flowering) which bring the cows into full milk. Other common Gaelic names for the Primrose are *Sabhaircín* and *Saorclann.*

To differentiate between the two plants: the cowslip has smaller leaves and its flowers grow in umbels, top-heavy and drooping, on long stems, while the bigger primrose flower has a stem to itself. Also, the cowslip tends to flower in mid-April, some three weeks later than its cousin and is more common in pastures while the primrose prefers banks and shady places. The yellow flowers of both were once widely used in English kitchens; and cowslip wine was especially prized.

We thought it better to warn those unfamiliar with wild flowers that the buttercup is a poisonous plant. It bears little or no resemblance to the cowslip or primrose, of course, but flourishes at much the same time, prefers the same habitat, and we once knew a novice who had collected a couple of quarts of them before someone stopped him. Later, he often wondered how he had picked that shiny, pollen-powdered, deep butter coloured brash flower – so, just in case, we warn you...

Any recipe for cowslips applies equally to primroses and there is no reason why you should not use both flowers in the same recipe. For the following recipes, it is best not to use the green stalks and lower parts of the plant, but only the yellow blossoms. If using dried flowers, only half the amounts given below are required.

COWSLIP WINE

A simple way to make very light Cowslip or Primrose Wine is to use a tightly-packed quart (1 litre) measure of the blossoms for each gallon (4½ litres) of boiling water and soak for two to three days, stirring and pressing every day. Strain into a fermenting jar, mix in 3 lb (1½ kg) sugar and 1 tspn. yeast and ferment to a finish. Syphon and bottle.

Here is a more full-blooded recipe:

1 gallon (4½ litres) cowslip blossoms
1 gallon (4½ litres) boiling water
3 lb (1½ kg) sugar
1 tbspn. cold tea
1 or 2 oranges
1 or 2 lemons
1 Campden tablet
1 tspn. yeast

Grate the rinds of the oranges and lemons, but make sure no pith is included. If using only one of each fruit you may like to include the juice with the rind. Add to the blossoms and pour the boiling water and sugar on them. When cool, include the Campden tablet. Some put in the yeast at this stage also, leaving the mixture to settle for forty-eight hours before straining. It is then said to be drinkable after three or four weeks or ready for bottling in two months. Fair enough if you are in a hurry, and have a little drop of spirits to add to it, but we prefer to go to a little more pains, i.e. leave for two days, stirring lightly occasionally, then strain, adding the yeast when cool and continuing in the usual way.

COWSLIP SYRUP

12 oz (350 g) cowslip blossoms
1 pint (½ litre) boiling water
½ lb (250 g) sugar

Pour the boiling water on the blossoms and leave standing for twenty-four hours. Strain and stir in the sugar. Boil gently until the infusion has the consistency of syrup. Its taste is remarkably similar to that of honey and it is delicious spread on bread or on hot, buttered scones.

COWSLIP TEA

1 oz (25 g) cowslip blossoms **1½ pints (¾ litre) boiling water**

This drink was taken both as a tonic and for its soothing effect. As our old eighteenth century *Herbal* says: 'Let it stand half an hour in a close vessel... To be drunk in the same manner as tea.' However, we treat tea in a different manner today, so simply serve the infusion cool and sweetened to taste. Primrose may be used instead of cowslip.

Since this book was first published the number of cowslips and primroses in the wild have decreased considerably, in fact in Northern Ireland and Great Britain the cowslip is a protected species. If you would like to use any of the above recipes why not grow the plants yourself. They are now commercially available as seed - no need to pick from the wild.

CRAB APPLE

Malus sylvestris

Unmistakably an apple tree, even when very bushy. It may grow up to 20 ft (6 m) in height and will usually be thickly branched. The true Crab has its share of dwarf shoots which turn into spines or thorns. The leaves are oval, toothed, sharp-pointed, often downy and grow on long stalks. As a rule, the apples are small, round, bright green or yellow green but may often be streaked with scarlet.

Craobha breágh' glasa ag seilt meala le h-áthas,
Clóbhar le fágháil ann go hárd ar gach taobh,
Úbhla i mbarr crann ann ag lúbadh le fána,
'S níor thuirse leat ráithe ann ag piocadh súgh-chraobh.

Fine green branches pouring nectar in joy, clover for the taking high on all sides, crab apples on the tree-tops, swinging down and down, and you wouldn't agree you'd grow tired of a season spent picking raspberries.
Raifterí (1784-1835)

Crab apples are the origin of – and often the stock on which – all cultivated apples are grown. They have been cultivated in these islands from time immemorial – even the English, who have schooled themselves to believe that just about everything in Britain was introduced by the Romans and then was reintroduced by the Normans, accept that crab apples were cultivated long before the advent of Julius Caesar. 'It is true', wrote T. W. Sanders (*Fruit and its Cultivation*, 1909), 'the Romans may have introduced some of their favourite kinds, but there is little doubt that the Ancient Britons cherished the apple both for food and beverage purposes. In proof of this, we have the fact that the Romans, when visiting Somerset, discovered a town bearing the name Avallonia, which existed on the site of Glastonbury. The meaning of this ancient British word is 'apple orchard', and hence it is assumed that orchards of apples existed in the district. We further learn that, when the Britons retreated... to Brittany, they esteemed their apple trees so highly that they carried them with them.'

Anyone with the barest knowledge of Celtic mythological legends will be struck by the numerous references to and associations with apples. Not only in Arthurian and Ossianic or *Fiannaíocht* tales will the significance of the apple be noted but in other myths, most notable, perhaps, being those concerned with the Celtic Isles of the Blest. To these, heroes were seduced by fairy maidens bearing apples (shades of Adam and Eve?). Beautiful apple trees blossomed there, yielding single fruits with a guarantee of one hundred years of life. We facetiously compare 'an apple a day keeps the doctor away...' Apples are mentioned in early Irish poetry and place-names such as Aghowle (Co. Wicklow) or 'the field of apples', Oulart (Co. Wexford) or 'the orchard', Knockullard (Co. Carlow) or 'the orchard-hill' are not uncommon, especially on the south-east coast of Ireland.

The Irish Gaelic for the fruit is *fiadh-ubhall* or *ubhall fiadháin*, wood or wild apple. The most common name in these islands, 'crab' and its variants, is almost certainly of Scandinavian origin. English *apple*, Welsh *afal* and Gaelic *ubhall* are obviously related but the origin of the root is uncertain.

Crab apples tend to vary a great deal in size, colour and taste, for the fruit is not only a variable species but (as with the wild plums) has crossed with many of the domesticated species gone wild. The true tree is small, deciduous, with broad, short, pointed leaves and dark, rough, knotty branches and trunk. The flowers are a typical apple blossom, growing in clusters. The fruit is generally yellowish green, often with a good red blush, and nearly always so sour as to be inedible raw. But it makes probably the finest jelly of all and verjuice (a forerunner of vinegar) and, of course, cider as well as apple wine. In general, the crabs need not be either peeled or cored and windfalls need not be overlooked.

CRAB APPLE JELLY

Crab apples	**Cinnamon or clove to taste, if desired**
Sugar	**Juice of 1 lemon for flavouring, if desired**

Crab apple jelly is traditionally acclaimed as the best jelly of all. Chop crabs into quarters or smaller (do not peel or core), cover with water to level of fruit and cook until pulpy. Strain overnight through a jelly bag, measure the juice and add 1 lb (500 g) warmed sugar for each pint (½ litre) of juice, dissolve, boil rapidly for about forty minutes stirring occasionally, by which time it should set when tested. Skim and proceed as advised in the section on jelly making.

CRAB APPLE AND BLACKBERRY JELLY

1 lb (500 g) crab apples
2 lb (1 kg) blackberries
Sugar

Wash and cut the crabs in half. Cook fruits separately, barely covering with water. When tender, strain through a jelly bag. Mix the juices and measure, add 1 lb (500 g) of sugar to each pint (½ litre) of juice. Bring slowly to the boil and stir in heated sugar, until dissolved. Boil rapidly until the mixture sets when tested. Skim and proceed as advised in the section on jelly making. You may care to add the juice of half a lemon to the above ingredients. To spice, include cloves and half a cinnamon stick, and to each pint (½ litre) of juice add 1 tablespoon of vinegar.

CRAB APPLE AND ELDERBERRY JELLY

1 lb (500 g) crabs
2 lb (1 kg) elderberries
Sugar
Cinnamon stick for spicing

Cut the crabs in half and put in saucepan with enough water to about three-quarter cover them. Simmer for about fifteen minutes. Add berries and bruise down with a wooden spoon. Add, if required, cinnamon. Cook until fruit is pulpy. Stain through a jelly bag and to each pint (½ litre) of juice allow 14 oz (425 g) sugar. Bring slowly to the boil and stir in heated sugar until dissolved. Boil rapidly until sets when tested. Skim, and proceed as advised in the section on jelly making.

CRAB APPLE AND ROSEHIP JELLY

3 lb (1½ kg) crabs
1 lb (500 g) hips
Juice of 1 lemon may be added, if desired
Sugar
2 pints (1 litre) water

Cook the hips to a pulp with half the water and the lemon juice. Wash the apples and cut them into slices without peeling or coring them. Cook them separately with the rest of the water until tender. Strain the juices together through a jelly bag taking great care as always with hips to prevent fibres from getting into the juice (see page 42). Measure, reheat slightly, add the warmed sugar at the rate of 1 lb (500 g) sugar per pint (½ litre) of juice. Stir until the sugar is dissolved. Boil rapidly for ten minutes or until the mixture sets when tested. Skim and proceed as advised in the section on jelly making.

CRAB APPLE AND ROWANBERRY JELLY *(1)*

2 lb (1 kg) crabs
3 lb (1½ kg) rowanberries
2 pints (1 litre) water, *i.e. this should be enough to just cover the fruit.*
Juice of 2 lemons
Sugar

Remove stalks from rowans and wash. Core the crabs and cut into quarters. Simmer rowans and crabs steadily in water until quite soft (probably for one hour or over). Strain through a jelly bag. Then boil liquid for about twenty minutes and add the warmed sugar, stirring until dissolved. Bring to the boil again stirring all the time. Add the lemon juice. Boil rapidly for ten minutes or until mixture sets when tested. Skim and proceed as advised in the section on jelly making. If cultivated apples are used instead of crabs, cider should be used instead of water.

CRAB APPLE AND ROWANBERRY JELLY *(2)*

2 lb (1 kg) crabs
2 lb (1 kg) rowanberries
Sugar
2 pints (1 litre) water
1 lemon

This recipe is for a very tart jelly. Simmer fruit until tender with 2 pints (1 litre) water and juice of the lemon, or the whole lemon sliced. Strain, add 1¼ lb (600 g) sugar per pint (½ litre) of juice. Proceed as in previous recipe.

CRAB APPLE AND SLOE JELLY

5 lb (2½ kg) crabs
3 lb (1½ kg) sloes
Sugar
Water

Wash and cut the crabs (neither coring nor peeling them), remove stalks from sloes and put the two fruits in the saucepan. Barely cover with water, cook gently until the sloes burst and the crabs are pulpy. Strain, measure, and to each pint (½ litre) of juice, add 1 lb (500 g) warmed sugar. Stir over a low heat until the sugar dissolves, boil quickly until it sets when tested. Skim and proceed as advised in the section on jelly making. If the mixture might seem too tart for your taste, use in proportions by weight of 1 sloes to 4 apples, or even as little as 1 to 7.

VERJUICE

Verjuice is a very old kind of vinegar made from the juice of the crab apple. The apples should be left on the trees for as long as possible without being exposed to severe frost and should be piled in a heap in a shady room, as is done for cider. When they have begun to sweat, it is time to remove the very bad fruit and crush the rest with a wooden mallet. The juice is collected (see section on cider making) and bottled, and left in a cool place for some weeks before use. Verjuice is really a slightly fermented (and very sharp) cider.

CRAB APPLE CIDER

Cider is made from the pure juice and the aromatic flavour of the crushed pips of the crab apple; strictly speaking, no sugar should be used. Without an apple press, the extraction of the juice is a fairly difficult business. We must confess that we have never found cider making anything but a chancy business and, consequently, have turned more and more to apple wine. The tradition of cider making has not been anywhere near as strong in Ireland as in England – not since the Celtic era, at any rate. Parts of Limerick and Clare had a fairly strong tradition until recent times and the following information was gleaned from a Clare man whose excellent cider we have drunk. He uses mature cooking apples, leaving them in a warm barn to mellow for a fortnight before crushing them in an adapted mangle (he has tacked thin laths of wood on the rollers to make crude cogs) and placing a heavy weight on the pulp to extract as much juice as possible. He leaves the juice to ferment in a warm room and to clear, before removing to a cooler atmosphere and fermenting to a finish.

Here is a method in more detail, which has much to recommend it. Plus 20 lb (10 kg) of crab apples are crushed in an apple press to give a gallon (4½ litres) of juice. These should have remained on the trees for as long as possible without being exposed to severe frost. They should be stored in heaps in a shady room until December. It is generally recommended that the water be cold, even somewhat frosted, when cider is being made: this prevents too rapid a fermentation. The pulp is exposed to the air for some hours and turned once or twice before pulp is processed and the juice runs into the container. Some home winemakers recommend at this point that sugar be added so as to get a hydrometer reading of 1.050 Specific Gravity, and then nutrient and ½ teaspoonful of yeast be included twenty-four hours later. We do recommend some use of sugar with crabs. At 70°F (21°C) there should be a very fast fermentation at first, and the juice will almost certainly froth over, so have the jar standing in a basin to prevent a mess. Do not bother to fit an airlock until this initial frenzy has slowed down; place a saucer or something similar on top of the jar. Top up and fit an airlock when ready. Cider should be allowed to clear itself before being syphoned off into a cask and left to ferment in a cool place. Syphon or rack off into another container when the fermentation obviously seems to have ceased and the cider is bright and clear beneath the scum on the surface. If a scum collects a second time, the cider is again racked off before bottling in the early spring.

Pulping and crushing may present problems. There are proprietary pieces of equipment, pulpers, presses, on the market. At the beginning, at least, few of us may wish to buy these but a little ingenuity may be brought to the rescue. You may already have a juice extractor which may do the trick if the apples are cut up small before being placed in the machine. The ordinary domestic mincer (No. 2 cutter) should also prove itself and the resulting pulp is then strained and squeezed. These may not always be successful as contact with metal may contaminate the juice. We have also heard of enterprising people who have improvised presses of strong timber and powered them with a car jack.

Remember that if fermentation has not finished, there is every chance that your cider will become re-activated in the warmer spring weather. This means that bottles are liable to burst – or, on opening, (less hazardous but very amazing) most of the drink will wind up in your eye and on the ceiling instead of in a glass.

CRAB APPLE THIRST QUENCHER

The term 'Applejack', as used in the United States, denotes a very potent apple 'brandy', distilled from fermented apple wine; in Ireland, any time we have heard the term used, it is applied to a non-alcoholic or very mildly alcoholic refreshment. Sweetened and diluted with water, we found it to be an excellent thirst quencher for the children.

8 lb (4 kg) crab apples
2 gallons (9 litres) water
Cloves if liked
8 lb (4 kg) sugar
3 lemons or pieces of bruised ginger

Crush the unpeeled crabs as well as possible, pour the water over them, cover with a cloth in the usual way and leave for a fortnight. Be warned that if boiling water is used on apples, so much pectin will be released into the must that it is virtually impossible to clear. On the other hand, if you have no apple press, you may opt for using boiling water to help break down the fruit; we have found that the difference between clear and unclear apple drink is, to a great extent, noticed more by the eye than by the tongue. Squeeze the apples daily. Strain and add cloves, etc. Stir well to dissolve the sugar. Syphon or rack off for cider (see previous recipe). Bottle (screw-capped cider bottles are best), leaving the caps loose for a few days; do not prime the bottles. Store in the usual cool, dark place for at least three months; it is wise to put the bottles in cardboard boxes.

CRAB APPLE WINE *(1)*

A very old method modernised to make a light, very dry and somewhat cloudy apple wine with as little trouble as possible. Slice and crush as much as feasible, 10 lb (5 kg) apples and put into 6 pints (3 litres) of boiling water (with Campden tablet). When cool, sprinkle on and stir in a teaspoonful of pectin-destroying agent and a little less yeast; a Champagne yeast culture, if you have it, is often suggested. Leave in the covered container for three days, bruising down the cap a couple of times or more a day. Strain and press the pulp with a heavy weight to collect as much juice as possible. Continue fermentation for three days before racking or syphoning. The wine (which will need further racking) is said to be drinkable after a fortnight; be wary about bottling it now, of course. Modern palates as a rule find this recipe too bitter. There are two things you may do to sweeten: (i) melt sugar or honey in a little warm water and add it when cool to your drink; (ii) add in some 2½ lb (1¼ kg) sugar in the usual way when making, remembering that this will necessitate a much longer period of fermentation. You might also feel like trying ½ lb (250 g) raisins along with the sugar.

It seems likely that in olden days people were not too fussy about whether their apple wine was cloudy or not. Today, most authorities would advise only *cold* water with apples. If you are not worried and have no good way of crushing the fruit, you are probably well advised to go ahead and use boiling water.

CRAB APPLE WINE *(2)*

10 – 12 lb (5 – 6 kg) crabs
6 pints (3½ litres) water
Yeast culture
3 lb (1½ kg) sugar
Nutrient (ammonium phosphate)

This is a much more sophisticated method and we give it because it includes a culture of good wine yeast (Champagne), which may be obtained from a home-brew supplier. The method may be applied to all other wines in this book. To make the yeast starter, merely follow the simple instructions on the packet. After a handful of days, your yeast culture should be active and you may now turn your attention to the other ingredients. Ideally, the crab apples should be allowed to mellow in the manner described in the section on Cider.

Putting the apples in a strainer, dip into a saucepan of boiling water for a few seconds. This not only kills the wild yeast but is very important when the attempt is being made to ferment 'on the skin.' Add the sugar and a tiny pinch of ammonium phosphate (a nutrient to help feed the yeast) to the apples, followed by the water, warm but not boiling. Stir to dissolve the sugar and leave to cool to room temperature 65°F (18°C); it is best to leave the must overnight as usual. Stir in the yeast culture, which you have previously prepared, and leave for a week, stirring two or more times each day. Strain (you may squeeze the pulp if you wish) and allow to ferment to a finish – usually about six to eight weeks. Rack or syphon and leave to mature and clear. As usual, make sure there is only a little air between the wine and the fermentation lock; top up with water if necessary. Rack or syphon again after eight weeks and bottle.

You may find the result too bitter for your taste. Put sugar in a bottle, add a little of the wine and shake to dissolve before pouring back into the container. It is important to drink this soon after, otherwise fermentation may begin again. Probably the best thing is to sweeten the entire lot to taste and return to the fermentation jar.

CRAB APPLE AND BLACKBERRY MOUSSE

See under Blackberry and Apple Mousse (page 63).

CRAB APPLE AND BLACKBERRY PUDDING

See under Blackberry and Crab Apple Pudding (page 64).

DANDELION

Leontodon taraxacum

A variable plant up to about a foot (30 cm) high which has characteristic flower heads, leaves and stems. The leaves are deeply toothed, the yellow-orange flower heads have more than a hundred tiny tongue-shaped florets and the tubular stems have a milky sap. On the top right (overleaf), the puff-ball, with its seeds and hairy parachutes, is illustrated; at upper left of centre is a mature flower head, while below we show two different stages in the life of the flower.

Cá bhfuil an luibh nach bhfásann
Tré thaltaibh Bhéal a' Ghártha? –
An casruadhán, an slánlus,
Cruadhphádraig a's leabhach bhuidhe...

Where is the herb that doesn't grow
through the lands of Belangare?
– dandelion, ribworth, plantain
and marshmallow...
Raifterí (1784-1835)

It is quite possible that many more people would have recognised the plant treated in this chapter if we had called it Pissybed or Piss-the-bed or Pee-the-bed or one of the many similar names found in these islands. Indeed the French call it *Piss-en-lit* as well as the more respectable *Dent dc Leon,* from which comes the English corruption, dandelion. All this serves to remind us that it has been used extensively as a diuretic medicine; as an old herbal book, quoting a Dublin recipe of the herb and roots, states, it is 'an excellent medicine for bad livers, and the dropsy'.

It is a pity that in debased folk-tradition this aspect of the plant has been exaggerated out of all proportion and people have come to fight shy of it. In fact, the dandelion was, perhaps, the most important of the more profuse herbs and has been used in medicine, cooking and drinks for a very long time.

There is evidence to show that it was cultivated in medieval monasteries, such as Holy Cross Abbey in Co. Tipperary. It figured prominently in the diet of the times, the leaves being used as a salad, the root as a vegetable, the flowers for wine-making. Add to this its medicinal use as a blood purifier and a remedy in heart disease, as a sleep inducer and appetiser; the Irish name, *caisearbhán*, probably refers to the juice which was taken in milk as a spring tonic. The root was also used in making a beer and a 'coffee', the leaves for fodder and chicken feed and even tobacco. One could go on, it seems, indefinitely, listing the traditional properties of the humble Piss-the-bed.

We have alluded to its international commercial possibilities in the introduction; but, though it is cultivated in the U.S.A., France and Japan, in these islands it is still generally looked upon as a noxious weed. Although our Brook's *New Family Herbal* states that the dandelion is 'another of our wild plants too common to need much description', two centuries later, we feel that it is necessary to describe it in some detail. The plant is widespread and abundant all over these islands in pastures and gardens and hedgerows. It flowers from early spring to early winter but is especially noticeable in April and May; do not wait until June to pick the blossoms as, almost overnight, they may turn to puff-balls of seed. The long leaves grow from the base of the plant and are deeply indented (hence the French name, 'lion's teeth'). The hollow stalks grow from 6 to 10 inches (15 – 25 cm) high and are crowned with a single distinctive flower, large, blazing yellow and comprised of a great quantity of petals. A bitterish but not unpleasant milky juice is to be got from each part of the plant, especially the root and hollow stems.

You may be surprised at the addition of cream of tarter in one of our recipes but the taste of dandelion concoctions has been improved in this manner for more than two centuries. Probably most people have heard of dandelion wine, though the practice of making it is nowhere near as common as it once may have been. Dandelion tea and beer was drunk throughout these islands, but it has been our experience to find the beer better known in the northern part of Ireland than in the south. Both root and leaves (cook them like spinach and serve with plenty of butter) have been much used as a vegetable and used in soup along with nettles and sorrel and other young spring herbs and leaves. If you find them a little too bitter for your taste, try blanching them in boiling water. The leaves go well in any salad (they need plenty of seasoning) but try mushrooms and watercress and a little garlic with them for a change. Many people will enjoy the leaves in a sandwich (especially with wholemeal bread or soda bread). One of the great advantages of the leaves is that, like water-

cress, they can be had most of the year round. Incidentally, we believe that St. George's Day, April 23rd, was the traditional day in England for making dandelion wine.

DANDELION BEER

½ – 1 lb (250 – 500 g) dandelion plants
1 – 2 lb (500 g – 1 kg) sugar
1 tspn. yeast
1 – 2 lemons
1 gallon (4½ litres) water
1 oz (25 g) cream of tartar
½ oz (10 g) root ginger

From the beginning of March until late spring is the best time for preparing this. The entire plant (leaves, stem, roots and indeed petals, if any) is used. Boil with the water, ginger and the rind of the lemon (but without the white pith) for no more than a quarter hour; strain and add to the sugar and cream of tartar. Leave, perhaps overnight, to cool to room temperature, add the yeast and the lemon juice. Ferment for three days, strain, bottle in screw-capped bottles and leave these for a week in a *cool* place. If stored in too warm a place or left for too long a time, fermentation will continue to such a degree that all kinds of exciting things may happen as you attempt to open the bottle. Alternatively, you may leave the beer in the fermentation jar for a longer period, but, of course, while gaining potency, it will tend to lose its 'jizz' and may become too 'flat.' Remember too, that this kind of beer will not keep at all well, as compared with wines. Sometimes it may happen that fermentation has not proceeded as it ought to have done during the three days, so that, on opening the bottles, the 'beer' merely tastes like a fruit squash. You may still convert this to beer by stuffing the necks of the bottles with cotton wool and removing to a warm place to encourage further fermentation.

DANDELION WINE

1 gallon (4½ litres) dandelion flower heads
3 lb (1½ kg) sugar
3 lemons (or 2 lemons and an orange)
1 gallon (4½ litres) water
½ - 1 lb (250 - 500 g) raisins (optional)
½ oz (10 g) root ginger (optional)
½ oz (10 g) cream of tartar (optional)
1 tspn. yeast

Pour the boiling water over the flowers and, after not more than three days, strain. Add the juice and rind (but not the white pith) of the citrus fruits, plus the bruised raisins and the other optionals. (Discretion, borne of experience, will enable you to deal with optional items so as to suit your own taste; we prefer not to over-use raisins, especially, in any of our wines, believing that they take from the distinctness of the wild flavours.) Add sugar, make sure it has completely dissolved before straining. Add half the yeast and leave for a week or less, squeezing at least once every day. Strain and place with the rest of the yeast in the fermentation jar. Ferment to a finish, rack and mature; like all wines, it will improve immensely if left to mature for a year or so before bottling.

DANDELION SYRUP

6 oz (150 g) dandelion flowers
6 oz (150 g) sugar
⅔ pint (400 ml) water

Pour the boiling water onto the dandelion flowers and leave standing for twenty-four hours. Strain and add the sugar. Bring to the boil and boil gently until the infusion has reached the consistency of syrup. Bottle and sterilize (see page 40). This makes enough to fill a small-sized mineral-water bottle. As picking dandelions may often be a tedious business and the making of the syrup so simple, we make several small quantities of the syrup at intervals from mid-March on as it is in great demand in our house on hot buns.

DANDELION COFFEE

This renowned caffeine-free coffee substitute is best prepared in autumn when the roots are surprisingly long and fat. The roots only are used. There is no need to try to peel them but, of course, they must be well cleaned. They may be left to dry in the open if the weather is very good but, to get the real coffee taste, we find it better to roast them in the oven until they are well-browned and brittle ('toasty'). Grind like ordinary coffee. If you have not got a coffee-grinder, mortar and pestle will do perfectly or simply use a rolling-pin.

Why not try crushed dandelion root in Gaelic Coffee? Heat a whiskey glass, pour in a shot of genuine Irish whiskey and add two teaspoonfuls of sugar. Now fill to near the brim with strong, hot 'dandelion coffee', stir to dissolve sugar and top off with whipped cream. No further stirring is done, the coffee and whiskey being drunk *through* the cream.

DULSE

Rhodymenia palmata

Tough, flat-stalked, brownish-red weed of the middle shore, growing up to 18 inches (45 cm) in length.

At the ould Lammas Fair, boys,
were ye ever there?
At the ould Lammas Fair
In Ballycastle-o?
Did ye ever treat yer Mary Anne
to a dulse and yella-man,
At the ould Lammas Fair in Ballycastle-o?
Traditional Song, 19th cent.

Dulse is a seaweed found on rocks at low tide, more especially on the coasts of Ireland and of Scotland. As the verse of the song indicates, it was dried and sold in the past and still may be bought, though (Ballycastle Lammas Fair excepted) not as easily as hitherto. It is a brownish-red in colour and grows to about 1½ ft (½ m) in size. The English name is from the Gaelic *duileasc* and indeed it is more often called dilisk or dilesk in Ireland.

Dulse, as all seaweed, should be washed well in cold water. It may be eaten raw and included in salads. Dried, it may be eaten as a savoury or used as a relish and in fish soup or sauce. It requires a lot of simmering – an hour or more – as a vegetable; the dried weed should first of all be soaked for three hours in water, then simmered in stock or milk until tender. After straining, reheat with the addition of a good-sized knob of butter and season with pepper. A good white sauce will enhance dulse as a vegetable. It was often included in coastal areas in the traditional Irish mashed-potato dishes and may also be cooked in the same way as laver (*porphyra umbilicalis*), the seaweed which is more often known as sloke in Ireland.

Try simmering the dulse in a little water until soft (this takes patience and a watchful eye to see that it does not burn). Roll in oatmeal when mushy. This 'bread' will keep for several days. Fry in bacon fat. The genuine laverbread is, of course, much prized in south-west Wales.

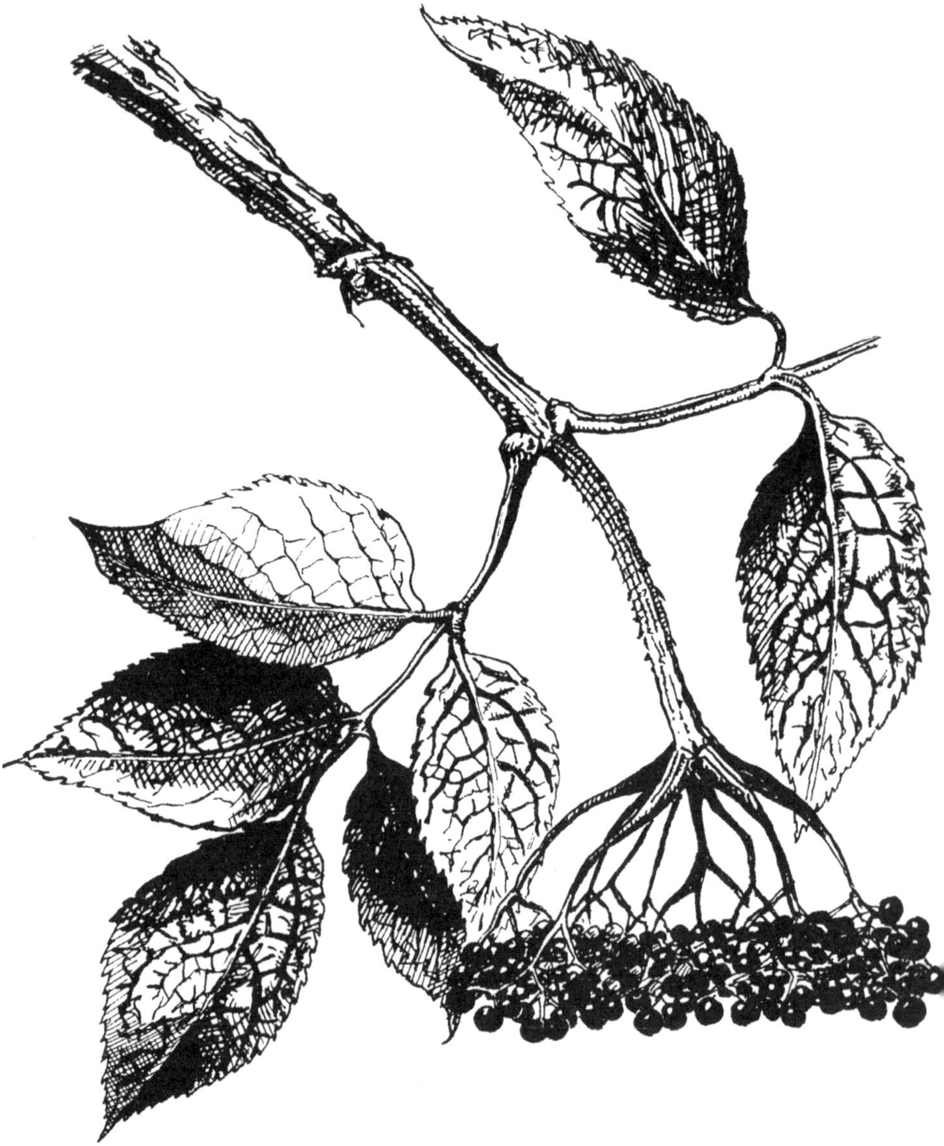

ELDER

Sambucus nigra

Usually an untidy, many-stemmed shrub, rarely more than 15 ft (4½ m) in height. The bark is corky, warty and grey-white, with the younger branches a freckled light brown. The shoots have a thick pith. There are 5 - 7 leaflets, each large, finely toothed and elliptical, dark green above and with distinctive tracery - and a sour smell. But its profuse heads of tiny, creamy white flowers have to be seen - and smelt - to be believed, while its often equally profuse heavy-hanging clusters of purple-black berries are a goodly sight.

There are many superstitions attached to the elder and most of them are not very nice. It is supposed to have been the tree from which the True Cross was made, the tree on which Judas hanged himself (which is why, at Eastertime, it has such a bad smell!) and so on. Too often it is looked upon with disfavour in these islands – except in those parts with strong Scandinavian (or 'Danish') traditions; in Scandinavia, it was once held sacred and, indeed, retains a good deal of its old respect to this day.

To be quite frank, from October until early Summer it is a ghastly-looking bush. By the end of May, it undergoes an amazing metamorphosis: its large, dark, serrated leaves (in groups of five) and masses of pale-green buds hide its skeleton-like branches, scaly trunk and 'Judas Ears' (a fungus seen to resemble the human ear and once much used for its medical properties). By mid-June, it is laden with masses of creamy flower clusters, which permeate the area with their characteristic scent, which reminds one of muscatel wine. (Some find the scent a little sickly, but we have always relished it and see in it a real symbol of mid-summer.) Our best successes with wine have been made from these flowers; we cannot recommend elderflower wine too highly, believing that if it has been properly prepared and matured it can hold its own with virtually any of the Continental white wines. Be warned, however, that the flower quickly gives way to the green berry: pick in the last two weeks of June or in the early first days of July to avoid disappointment.

The flowers have many uses in herbal medicine, including the once renowned 'Rob of Elder' used for 'causing a sweat in cases of cold and violent rheumatic afflictions.' Do not wash the flowers, as this robs them of much of their quality;

check them for insects, however. As with rowanberries, take the entire cluster when picking; the stalks – the main ones at any rate – are usually removed when preparing the wine, or whatever else is required.

Depending on the weather, elderberries may ripen in August. They ought to be a deep red-black. If not yet ripe, they will taste bitter even if they look right. When the clusters turn upside down, it is usually a good sign, but we have found the odd year when the berries just refused to ripen (1973, for instance) and consequently the wine was of little value. On the other hand, and more often too, thanks be to Providence, the amount of good fruit is so immense that it has to be seen to be believed. Of course, we all *see* the fruit as the bush is so widespread and common on roadsides and hedgerows and elsewhere; unfortunately, in this 'consumer age', it just doesn't register with us that there is such a good and easily available source of food and drink about. It is known by several names, including Boortree and Judas Tree; we used to call it Boot Tree in the north-west when we were children. The Irish Gaelic is *Trom* and the berries *Caora Troim*; an older name in Ireland and Scotland was *Ruis*, which gave its name to the Gaelic letter R. Welsh *ysgaw* and English 'elder' (from Anglo-Saxon) both seem to refer to the hollow, smaller branches of the tree; so that, if for some reason or other, you are not too sure when identifying your tree, break off a branch to see if it has the soft, white pith, which (once upon a time, although not too long ago) assured that every schoolboy could arm himself with a pea-shooter.

Elderflowers, of course, make an excellent flavouring (remember it ought *not* to be washed): you may sprinkle them over salads, milk puddings or tarts. Cook them along with jams or jellies or puddings in a muslin bag which is removed before serving. Incidentally, there would seem to be some tradition that dried elderberries may have been used in such things as barm brack or 'curney cake' as a substitute for raisins.

ELDERBERRY SOUP *Serves 4–6*

1 lb (500 g) elderberries
2 pints (1 litre) water
Grated rind of lemon
Sugar
¾ oz (15 g) cornflour or potato flour

Clean the fruit and simmer with a little of the grated lemon rind in the water until soft. Add about 3 oz (75 g) of sugar, remembering that fruit soup should not be as sweet as a dessert. Blend the flour with a little water, stir into the soup, bringing to the boil again to thicken. Serve hot or chilled.

ELDERFLOWER BATTER / PANCAKES *Makes 24 pancakes*

Elderflower head or two
Honey or sugar
1 pint (½ litre) milk
½ tspn. salt
8 oz (225 g) flour
1 – 2 eggs
½ tspn. butter

Having mixed the lightly beaten egg(s) with the milk and melted butter, stir well into the sifted flour and salt. Let this stand for one hour at least. You may then proceed in either of two ways. You may strip the small flowers from the stalks and mix them into the batter, or you may dip the entire flower head into the batter, later cutting off the stalk by which it was held. In either case deep fry in hot fat or cooking oil until brown. They are best served with honey but of course sugar will do. You might like to experiment with extra flavouring, say lemon juice, or more traditional flavouring such as mint or fennel, etc.

ELDERBERRY SYRUP

This may be made in the same way as Blackberry Syrup (see pages 64, 65). However, when following Recipe 2, add up to half as much water again unless the fruit is very ripe and juicy. It is a good idea to include a few cloves to each pint (½ litre) of elderberry juice when adding the sugar, but these should be removed before bottling.

Elderberry syrup has always been famous as a basis for hot drinks to relieve winter coughs and colds. A very old recipe for syrup for this purpose simply states: 'Take of ripe elderberries five parts, of sugar one part; boil with a gentle heat to the consistence of thick honey.'

ELDERFLOWER AND GOOSEBERRY JAM

4 lb (2 kg) green gooseberries
16 elderflower heads
4 lb (2 kg) sugar
1½ pints (¾ litre) water

Top, tail and wash gooseberries. Place in saucepan with the water. Bring to the boil and simmer for about twenty minutes, by which time the berries should be tender without being reduced to a pulp. Add warmed sugar and stir over a low heat until it dissolves. Bring to the boil rapidly and at this point add the elderflowers tied in a muslin bag. When preserve is set, remove flowers, skim and proceed as usual.

ELDERBERRY AND BLACKBERRY JAM

Make in exactly the same way as Blackberry Jam with apple juice (page 65), except that elderberries are included with the blackberries in whatever proportions you wish. If it happens to be a year in which elderberries are not ripening well, you will of course use more of the blackberries and add sugar to taste.

ELDERBERRY BUNS

Make in the same way as Fraughan Buns (page 110).

ELDERBERRY AND BLACKBERRY CHUTNEY

Make in the same way as Blackberry and Elderberry Chutney (page 63).

ELDERBERRY AND CRAB APPLE JELLY

See under Crab Apple and Elderberry Jelly (page 85).

ELDERBERRY AND CULTIVATED APPLE JELLY

Make in exactly the same way as Blackberry and Cultivated Apple Jelly (page 67), merely substituting elderberry for the blackberry.

ELDERBERRY DRINK

As with the Blackberry Drink, elderberries may be simmered for a short while in water, strained and sweetened to taste. As they are a little deficient in acid, however, a little lemon juice is always a welcome addition. Otherwise, bruise and strain the fresh fruit to procure the juice, add three parts water to one juice, a little lemon, and sweeten to taste. By the way, you will have wasted your time if the berries are not absolutely ripe.

ELDERBERRY WINE

We always have a good laugh when we recall the first wine we ever made. It had been an exceptionally good year for elderberries and we collected an enormous amount, which we were using in sweets and drinks. One of us discovered a most sophisticated recipe for elder wine and set to work. But the business seemed so complicated and he was so meticulous about it that the other – no prizes for guessing who! – lost patience, grabbed some berries and sugar, borrowed a little yeast and – you guessed it! – she produced a wine far superior to the other. Despite attempting a few other recipes with varying success, we have tended to stick to the original down-to-earth formula, which we now give.

3½ lb (1¾ kg) elderberries fully ripe
1 tspn. yeast
1 gallon (4½ litres) water
1 – 2 tspn. lemon juice
2½ – 3 lb (1¼ – 1½ kg) sugar

Make sure all stalks are removed and boil the fruit in the water for ten minutes. Stir in the sugar and when cool enough add half the yeast. Leave to stand for three days, then strain into a jar and, having added the rest of the yeast, ferment to a finish. It is wise to test for too much dryness and add sugar accordingly. To assist fermentation, you may like to add up to ½ lb (250 g) chopped raisins and an additional three tablets of yeast nutrient to the must. It is also a good idea to include a Campden tablet. When fermentation is complete, syphon into bottles and leave for at least six months.

ELDERFLOWER THIRST QUENCHER

If you have never tasted a drink made from the elderflower, you will be tempted to do so if, next time they are in bloom, you sniff them and munch them straight off the branch. Incidentally, never wash elderflowers, as they will then lose much of their fragrance – just check to see that there are no insects in them and get rid of any by hand.

The simplest method is merely to put a few heads in a saucepan, pour boiling water on top of them, leave to cool before straining and add a little sugar, if required.

A more sophisticated drink is often known as Elderflower 'Champagne', although, in fact, experts can make an elderflower wine which closely resembles a real champagne.

7 – 10 heads of elderflower
2 tbspn. cider (or wine) vinegar
Juice and rind (without white pith) of 1 or 2 lemons
1½ lb (750 g) sugar
1 gallon (4½ litres) cold water

Put all the ingredients into a container, say, a polythene bucket. Stir until sugar dissolves, cover and leave for twenty-four hours, squeezing occasionally. Strain and bottle in screw-top bottles. It will be ready to drink in about three weeks but it keeps very well and tends to improve throughout the summer. Keep in a cool, dark place.

ELDERFLOWER WINE á la EILEEN

A friend called Eileen once gave us – by word of mouth – her recipe for Elderflower 'Champagne' (see previous recipe) but we got it mixed up and the result was a very light, very sweet and pleasant drink, more of a good thirst quencher than anything else.

7 – 10 heads of elderflower
1½ tbspn. cider vinegar
1 gallon (4½ litres) water
Juice and rind (without white pith) of 2 lemons
1¼ lb (600 g) sugar
yeast

Pour the boiling water over all the ingredients and add the yeast when the temperature is right. We use a good deal less than the usual quantity of yeast so that the wine may be given safely to younger folk and to those who usually 'fight shy' of alcoholic drinks. Ferment for four days, strain and leave until fermentation is nearly complete, i.e. until the wine has started to clear. Syphon until you have a clear bottle nearly full with the wine, plug the neck with cotton wool and put in quite a warm place to accelerate fermentation. If a heavy yeast deposit is to be seen at the bottom after a week or so, return to the fermenting jar, and try again a few days later. When the yeast deposit in the bottle is light, bottle all the wine in screw top bottles. This method will give you a frothy, champagne-like effect.

If the yeast deposit in the bottle has been quite heavy, fermentation still has a good way to go and the wine, if bottled, could burst its containers; always put bottles which contain sparkling wine in cardboard boxes so as to minimise the danger of flying glass. The beginner is probably best advised to ferment to a finish, until he learns to recognise a light deposit from a heavy one. This drink is absolutely delicious after a year. We have found that, at any time, this or any of the other elderflower 'thirst quenchers' go remarkably well with whiskey.

ELDERFLOWER WINE *(2)*

1½ pints (¾ litre) stripped elder blooms
1 gallon (4½ litres) boiling water
½ cup cider vinegar
1 tspn. yeast
2 pieces root ginger or 2 tbspn. ground ginger
3 lb (1½ kg) sugar
2 lemons
2 oranges
1 tbspn. cold tea

While checking in various sources, we have noted that just about every measure from ¾ pint (450 ml) to 3 pints (1½ litres) of the blossom per gallon (4½ litres) of water is recommended; we would never care to make do with less than 1½ pints (¾ litre) and have never had the patience to gather more than 2 pints (1 litre) per gallon (4½ litres). As for root ginger, as often as not when we wanted it for a certain recipe we hadn't got any in the house so we mixed in a teaspoon or two of ordinary ground ginger. We have used a little more cider vinegar, if we had it to spare, and less water, keeping the mixture to about a gallon (4½ litres) all told.

Wash and slice the lemons and oranges and put with the blooms, sugar and ginger in the bin or pail. Pour on the boiling water, the tea and the cider vinegar (if you have it) and, when cool enough, add the yeast. Strain after fermenting for four days. Some experts hold that yeast nutrient is necessary – and it certainly does no harm.

Strain into fermenting jar. When it clears, syphon or rack again. If you are still a novice, it is best to ferment to a finish, racking it again before bottling. As you gain in experience, you can try converting it into a sparkling wine with some of the 'jizz' of champagne by using the method given above in Elderflower wine *á la* Eileen.

FRAUGHAN / BLUEBERRY

Vaccinium myrtillus

An erect but small undershrub, rarely more than 9 inches (22 cm) which, often obscured by heather, may look more delicate than it actually is. The pointed, slightly toothed, oval leaves are bright green in summer but may tend to turn yellow (or even red) when the fruit has ripened. The hanging fruit is about the size of a blackcurrant, round and blue-black and often with a grey bloom of yeast.

A Shliabh Sneachta, nach aoibhinn duit
Ag éirighe amach ar maidin?
Is gur gile thú ná 'n fhaoileann,
Thig cíb ort agus canach.
Bídh áirní ar an fhraoich ann
'S sugh-craobh ar an abar
Is tobar glan fíor-uisge
Ón díleann in do mhullach.

O Snowy Mountain, isn't it grand for you as you rise out in the morning, and you brighter than the sea-gull in your sedge and bog-cotton. There are sloes on the heath (i.e. fraughans), there are raspberries on the peat, and a clear true-water spring from the floods upon your head.
Anon. Nineteenth century

It would seem that *Vaccinium myrtillus* has more local names in these islands than any other fruit: Fraughan (obviously from Gaelic *Fraochán*), Bilberry (from a Scandinavian root); Blueberry, Blaeberry (from a very ancient root, meaning 'blue', of Teutonic origin, this name is found mostly in northern Britain and northern Ireland); Whortleberry, and its derivatives Whorts, Herts, Hurts (from what would seem to be an Old English root, although the Gaelic *fraoch* 'heather' – is surely cognate). Wimberry (in England) and Whinberry (in Ireland) and Huckleberry (in America) are probably corruptions of Whortleberry. There are several other variations and also Cowberry (Scotland

and Ireland) and Crowberry (England and Ireland). We do not presume to even guess at what lies behind such a conglomeration of names: there is obviously the basis for a worthwhile thesis in the above list alone!

The American blueberry may have popularised that name on this side of the Atlantic by starring in the evergreen song, 'Blueberry Hill', but centuries before the berry had given a title to one of the most significant days in the Irish calendar of earlier times: Fraughan Sunday. The fraughan is the first of all the wild fruits to ripen and many people will recall that there used to be – in some parts there still is – a special day set aside in the early autumn to go to the hills for a day out, picking fraughans and, of course, courting: how much time was allocated to the different pursuits, we leave to yourselves to reckon. The day traditionally set aside for this was the Sunday closest to the first day of August. As Máire Mac Néill has pointed out in her monumental study of the ancient Celtic Festival, Fraughan Sunday is a remnant of the Festival of Lughnasa; Lugh, whose name is recalled in Lyon and London, was a Celtic God of the Sun. Throughout Ireland, Fraughan Sunday has been popularly known by many local names: Donagh Sunday or Crom Dubh's Sunday, *Domhnach na bhFear* (or 'The Men's Sunday'), Garlic Sunday and, perhaps best of all, Garland Sunday. To this day, it is the occasion of the huge penitential pilgrimage to St. Patrick's Mountain in Mayo, but there are still remnants of many local pilgrimages and social gatherings elsewhere in the country. The celebrations on Garland Sunday at St. Brigid's Well in Clare's Liscannor was, typically, both religious and social, a carnival day, with prayers, sports and tests of strength, and courting. The fraughan, the first fruits of the harvest, were eaten on that day, as were the first new potatoes (which is why it was sometimes known as The Sunday of the New Potatoes).

Unfortunately, through both clerical puritanism and real excesses, Fraughan Sunday is not what it used to be when we were young; but we cannot recommend anything more wholesome to townspeople in this day and age than that the entire family takes to the hills in time-honoured fashion and celebrates the bountiful Providence by picking fraughans – and by other, no less ancient, pursuits. Herein lies the stuff of life. Of course, you must first be able to recognise the plant – and the wise leader of the expedition ought to have surveyed the 'ground' thoroughly beforehand, because, like all good things in life, the fraughan, though fairly widespread, may not be all that easy to come by. There would seem to be more than one variety of the fruit (which might account for some of the many local variations in the names) but in general this small deciduous shrub grows to no more than 1½ feet (½ m) high. The leaves are bright green, oval and, on close inspection, are seen to be toothed. The flowers are small, solitary, pretty, urn-shaped, pinkish. The juicy berry is blue-black, about the size of a blackcurrant and usually covered in a whitish bloom. By mid-September, these will tend to be getting over-ripe. They are a very good source of ascorbic acid and citric acid; in other words, the quantity of Vitamin C is high.

The shrub is found in bogs, heaths, moors and even peaty woods, in fact wherever heather grows, but is not usually common on the south east coast of either Ireland or Great Britain. It is difficult to find, as often it will be concealed by heather – so it is advisable to search for it when the flowers are out. The fruit (which was once used in dyeing) is very fine. Many would say the jam and jelly made from them has a better quality than those made from blackberries and they are not as seedy. (By the way, fraughans require the addition of pectin, so add crab apples or lemon.) The syrup was used as a remedy for diarrhoea. It is surprising that it has never been commercially grown in these parts, especially in areas with acid soil. In days gone by, the berries found a ready market in the bigger towns in Britain, and Londoners especially esteemed them in tarts or fresh with cream and a good deal of sweetening.

Nowadays, the Americans are promoting the sale of their blueberries to British and Irish consumers, and we see that garden catalogues are beginning to 'push' the imported plants here. Will we ever learn?

FRAUGHAN SOUP

Make as for Elderberry Soup (page 100), but using somewhat less water. If you are a little finicky about skins and seeds, strain before adding the sugar.

FRAUGHAN AS A SWEET

To the modern taste the fraughan is probably a little too acid when eaten fresh with sugar and cream as blackberries often are. So it is probably best to stew them first of all.

BLUEBERRY PIE

We could hardly leave this out as it is the famed American national dish. Simply take the berries with about half their weight of sugar, sprinkle with a little lemon juice and bake in a pastry-lined pie dish with pastry cover in a moderate oven for approximately half an hour.

FRAUGHAN STEAMED PUDDING

Suet pastry
Sugar
Fraughans

Line a pudding basin with suet crust and fill with fraughans and sugar, at least 4 oz (125 g) sugar to 1 lb (500 g) berries and cover filling with more of the pastry. As with all puddings made from suet pastry, it should be covered with a cloth and steamed for at least two hours.

FRAUGHAN BUNS *Makes 20–24 buns*

1 large cup fraughans
½ lb (250 g) self-raising flour
2 oz (50 g) butter
1 egg
¼ pint (150 ml) milk
¼ lb (125 g) sugar
Pinch of salt

Mix the sugar, flour and salt and cut in the butter until just about blended. Add fraughans, the egg and the milk and stir quickly but not so much that the batter becomes runny. Pour at once into greased patty tins until three-quarters full. Bake at 400°F (200°C) Reg. 6 and check after a quarter of an hour. Remove straight away from tins. They should be served while still hot, but, if they have to be reheated, wrap them in tin foil before placing in oven.

FRAUGHAN JAM

Fraughan jam has of course always been a great favourite in Ireland and in Scotland but, the berry being very succulent and having little pectin, the jam will be far too runny unless certain precautions are taken. We suggest using the recipe for Blackberry Jam with Apple Juice (page 65) but using no water at all and cooking the apples carefully to extract the juice.

FRAUGHAN AND APPLE JELLY

For the reason mentioned above, it is best to use at least as much apples as fraughans. Make the same way as for Crab Apple and Blackberry Jelly (page 85), but keeping the amount of water to a minimum.

FRAUGHAN DRINK

See the notes on Blackberry and Elderberry Drinks. Friends of ours collect the juice by squeezing and straining and, having added soda water, sweeten to taste.

FRAUGHAN WINE

3 lb (1½ kg) fraughans
3 lb (1½ kg) sugar
1 tspn. yeast
1 gallon (4½ litres) water
1 tbspn. cold tea
8 oz (250 g) raisins (optional)

If you intend having a sweet wine, it is probably best to add the raisins, but cut back the weight of berries and sugar to 2½ lb (1¼ kg) each. Crush the fruit, pour on the boiling water and add the sugar. When cool, add in the yeast, tea and raisins. It is advisable not to ferment on the pulp for longer than three days (four at the outside) before straining into the fermenting jar and proceeding as usual. On the other hand, you may proceed as for Sloe Wine (pages 72 and 73), but do not leave for longer than three days fermenting on the pulp.

FURZE / WHIN

Ulex europeus

A dark-coloured evergreen, with stiff, sharp thorns instead of leaves. There are at least two main types, the smaller being 3 - 6 ft (1 - 2 m) high, the other (illustrated at bottom left) may reach a rank 12 ft (4 m). The bright yellow flowers have a typical pea-family form and a musky odour. The short, hairy, grey-blue pad is shown at top right.

This common evergreen bush is known by three different names, Furze, Whin and Gorse, among English-speakers in these islands. Gorse, from an Anglo-Saxon root, is unknown in some parts of England itself and Whin or even Whine, Norse derivations which we automatically expect to find in Scotland and in north and north-west of Ireland, is quite common outside those areas. Furze, also it seems to be from an Anglo-Saxon root, is probably the most usual name. The common Scots Gaelic is *droighneach*, thorny bush, and the Welsh *eithin* is obviously cognate with Irish *aiteann* and this would seem to refer to the blaze of colour when the bush is in full flower. It occurs in many Irish place-names north and south, e.g. Mullaghanattin or *Mullach an Aitinn* ('The Furze Hill-Top') in Co. Down. The whin, too, finds a place in topography; witness another place-name not too far away from the above, the quaintly sounding Whinney Knowes.

Botanists distinguish three different species but we feel it is open to question whether much of our present day bushes are not in fact intermediate forms. Two main varieties have been distinguished in Ireland in the past, *Aiteann Gaelach*, Gaelic or native furze, and *Aiteann Franncach*, *'French'* or foreign, exotic furze. Traditionally, the smaller bush is supposed to be the native; it has the darker flower and stronger scent and is at the height of its bloom in August and September. The big, rank bush, which grows taller than a man, has a lighter flower and blooms in February and March, is supposed to be the 'foreign' furze in Ireland. We have been told that it never grew on Rathlin Island off the coast of Antrim until a non-native called Gage sowed it there at the end of the eighteenth century. We are inclined to believe that the same is true for Britain as a whole and that *Ulex Europeus* proper only made its widespread appearance in these islands as an escape from cultivation and at much the same time as it invaded a large area in central Europe from its presumed homeland in France and the Iberian Peninsula.

A member of the *Leguminosae* or pea family, with sharp spines instead of leaves and wonderful yellow flowers which turn whole hillsides into a blaze of yellow and gold, it is abundant on barren soils. We have mentioned the spring and autumn flowerings but, of course, it never actually goes out of flower: even on the bitterest winter day the not-so-few flowers glitter triumphantly, which led to the English folk-saying that 'kissing is out of fashion when the gorse is out of bloom'.

In the not-so-distant past, the countryman made good use of furze. It was once deliberately cultivated as fodder – this surely accounts for the spread of the bigger bush – the young shoots being especially relished by horses and also eaten by cattle. Special mills were used to bruise the shoots, some of which, we are told, may still be seen in the Mourne area of Co. Down; they consist of huge timber mauls and granite blocks. Among other things, it provided kindling, bedding, dyes, hurleys and cures and – more important for us – tradition asserts that it brews one of the best of wines. In earlier times, the flowers were used to flavour whiskey.

Furze may have become something of a pest today for once it gains possession it is extremely difficult to extirpate and has formed dense cover over a vast area of moorland and hillside. Familiarity has bred contempt so it is well to remember the reaction of the famous Swedish botanist, Linnaeus, when he first saw it, in full flower on Wimbledon Common: he threw himself on his knees and thanked God for allowing him to see such beauty.

FURZEFLOWER WINE

½ – 1 gallon (2 – 4½ litres) furzeflowers
1 gallon (4½ litres) water
2½ – 3 lb (1¼ – 1½ kg) sugar
1 tbspn. cold tea
1 orange
1 lemon
2 oz (50 g) root ginger (optional)
1 tspn. yeast

Furzeflower wine is best, we feel, when rather dry. Try it first of all with a ½ gallon (2 litres) of flowers and a little ginger (see note on elderflower wine, page 105), later on, you may prefer to increase the quantity of flowers and decrease that of ginger. If you do, you will probably find also that one gallon (4½ litres) flowers requires 3 lb (1½ kg) or even more sugar.

Some winemakers advocate simmering the flowers (in a bag) in the water for about a quarter of an hour and then removing them altogether. We feel this is a reasonably good idea if you have gathered a gallon (4½ litres) of flowers or more. Being quite satisfied with the half gallon (2 litres), we merely cover the flowers, ginger, juice and rind (without white pith) of the fruit with boiling water. After five days, with occasional stirring, this is then strained into the fermentation jar; the sugar melted in the rest of the water (heated) is added and, when the lot is cool, in goes the yeast (and the yeast nutrient, if you like) and the cold tea. Ferment to a finish. It is a good idea to syphon after a couple of months and again in a further eight to ten weeks, if fermentation has been slow in this latter stage. The wine should, of course, be matured.

HAWTHORN

Crataegus monogyna

Often gnarled and twisted, this is the 'fairy-tree' of superstition, usually not more than 20 ft (6 m) in height and branching out from close to the ground. The older branches are ash-grey and it is, of course, a thorny bush. The small leaves are distinctly lobed, very dark green on the upper side and have a nutty flavour. The abundant deep-red haws (smaller than rose hips) are cream fleshed, with a single, big stone.

'When all fruit fails – haws!'

Perhaps nothing better indicates the changed attitude in this century to the wild harvest than the fact that so many folk-sayings connected with it have passed out of general use. Some generations ago, there were many such idioms and proverbs in both Gaelic and English. One such saying covered a situation wherein one was forced to rely on something which, while it sufficed, was not highly recommended: 'When all fruit fails – haws.' It must be all of twenty-five years since we heard that in a conversation.

It's not quite fair on the lowly haws, however. We have regularly made excellent haw wine and haw jelly. (Not everyone cares for the highly individual taste of the latter.) Many people have enjoyed eating haws raw from the trees. We feel, therefore, that the folk-saying refers not so much to their taste or quality but to the fact that their big stones and stubborn lower ends prove a nuisance. Perhaps it would be as well to mention that there is a common folk-belief that eating haws causes yellow jaundice: there is usually some truth behind the most ridiculous of folk-sayings, but we have made normal use of both haw wines and jellies and never suffered any discomfort. Without a doubt these are the most abundant wild fruit of all, so much so that in many areas they give the landscape a distinct glaze of red. They are smaller and neither so hard nor so shiny as the rose hips; their flesh is a creamy colour. The leaves, too have their uses. The youngest leaves are especially pleasant in a salad. Dried and incorporated with Speedwell, the little plant common in dry pastures, they were much used as a tea in medieval times – in Holy Cross, for instance.

The tree is also called the May Bush, especially in the month of May when its pure white blossom (sometimes pink-tipped) is really more spectacular than that of the imported Cherry tree so beloved by town planners and city councillors. It is no surprise then to learn that *Crataegus monogyna* is also commonly called Whitethorn in the earlier part of the Summer, thus causing many townspeople to think of Whitethorn and Hawthorn as two separate species. We knew that the light but delicious Hawthorn Blossom Wine was not uncommon in Britain in former times but had come across no reference to it in Ireland until recently when we learned that, about fifty years ago, it was made in one area at least – in the Newport district of north Tipperary (a name more synonymous with home-made whiskey than wines!).

In many parts of Britain the tree is often called a Quickthorn. Most country people in Ireland would probably refer to it as a Skeaghbush (from the Gaelic *Sceach Gheal* or 'bright thorn-bush') and the haws used to be known as skeehories (from *sceachóirí* or more correctly *sceach chaora*). The Welsh is *draen wen* ('white thorn') and also *ysbyddad.*

The whitethorn was part of the 'May' the farmer brought to his door to celebrate May Eve. There were many beliefs and superstitions attached to it. It was believed that the crown of thorns placed on the head of Christ was made from it; on the other hand, the 'fairy tree' or 'bishop's bushes' or 'lone bushes' so common in the Irish countryside are more often than not hawthorn. We saw one such bush some years ago at Knockmant, Co. Westmeath: it grew out of a dead oak tree and underneath it were the remains of three 'high priests', buried some 3,000 years ago.

HAWTHORN AND CRAB APPLE JELLY

1 lb (500 g) haws
2 lb (1 kg) crabs
Sugar
Juice of ½ lemon

We have found haws to be too dry to attempt to make jelly from them on their own. Crab apples go well with haws and we have been greatly pleased with the results of the following recipe, the children especially loving it on hot buttered scones. Wash and cut the crabs and place with the haws in saucepan with just enough water to cover them. Add lemon juice. Long simmering is needed. Strain and for every pint (½ litre) of juice add 1 lb (500 g) warmed sugar. Stir until sugar dissolves. Then boil rapidly until jelly sets when tested. Skim and proceed as advised in the section on jelly making.

HAWTHORN BLOSSOM LIQUEUR

A 1 lb (500 g) jar with a good sealing top – we have found Kilner jars ideal for this type of thing – is packed full with the flowers of the May and then covered with brandy or whiskey – a little patience is required here for as little air as possible ought to remain in the jar. Strain after a fortnight or so, squeezing out all the liquor. A tablespoon of sugar is carefully melted (with a drop or two of water) and, when cold, is added to the liquor and thoroughly stirred. Leave for a few hours (to see if it requires straining again) before bottling. It is ready to drink straight away.

HAWTHORN BLOSSOM WINE

Make in the same way as Furzeflower Wine (page 115) but do not include the ginger and increase the sugar to at least 3 lb (1½ kg). When transferring to the fermentation jar, a really good straining is advised.

HAW WINE

¾ gallon (3 litres) haws
1 gallon (4½ litres) water
6 oz (150 g) sultanas
Juice and rind (without white pith) of 2 lemons
2¾ lb (1¼ kg) sugar
Pectin-destroying enzyme
1 tspn. yeast

One of the most pleasant surprises we have ever had in winemaking was when we drank the wine of the haw for the first time. Some years, the berries are exceptionally fat and soft and these make the best wine. Pour the boiling water onto the haws, sultanas and lemon peels. When the must has cooled down, you may include the Campden tablet and pectin-destroying enzyme. Cover and leave for two days, squeezing with the hand twice a day. Now add the rest of the ingredients, including a yeast nutrient if you have it, and leave to ferment quickly for a further three to four days, but not more. Strain and ferment to a finish, adding sugar if necessary to prolong the process. Mature.

HAZEL

Corylus avellana

The bush is from 4 to 15 ft (1¼ – 4½ m) high but generally tends to be on the smaller side. The bark is brown-red and grey, shiny and smooth but inclined to peel; the leaves are round, ribbed and finely toothed, the nuts small, oval, enclosed in thick green husks. A cluster of three nuts is illustrated, but there may be two to five.

The fact that hazel branches were included in the 'Summer' brought into the house on May Day (see notes on Hawthorn and Cowslip) reminds us that, long ago, people ate a great deal more of the nuts than we do today. The numerous references to them in earlier Gaelic and Welsh poetry seems to indicate that these *collchnónna* provided a not inconsiderable source of food in the Celtic diet, at any rate. So well they might, for – as vegetarians well know – they contain a great deal of protein. The English once cultivated the hazel and it is still, of course, much cultivated on the Continent and in the Middle East. The tree itself was once highly thought of, being used in hurdles and baskets, as handles of farm implements and in making flails, and for springles or *scoilb* in thatching, for water-divining and, indeed, warding off evil. In England, it was used in the making of charcoal, for forge-work and for sketching. It grows abundantly in tolerably dry areas throughout these islands. It is a small tree, which grows up to 12 feet (4 m) or so in height. It has a brownish-red, smooth bark, which is inclined to shine and peel. The leaves are short and broad, indented and downy in spring. The nuts, encased in thick, green husks, are ready for picking in mid-autumn. As children, we often kept them to ripen indoors in jam jars, on a window-ledge where they could get the sun; unfortunately, at Hallowe'en, the great traditional time for eating them, many had become mouldy or the kernels had shrivelled up. It was held that this used to be a result of too much warmth, but probably arose from the fact that the nuts were packed in damp weather.

Those country people who were wise in folkways had a different method. Nuts were gathered in small sacks on a *dry* day, after mid-autumn or later when they were so ripe as to tend to fall. The green husk was scrupulously removed and any nuts showing signs of mould, with dark or grey shells, were discarded. The sack was then kept in a dry, airy place (not necessarily a warm place) and every so often the nuts would be spilled out, those growing mouldy removed and the others returned to the sack. (Incidentally, air-tight bags are *not* recommended.) You will probably lose many nuts with this method; in the old days, so much would have been picked that this did not really matter. We are inclined to think that there must have been a fool-proof method of maturing and preserving hazel nuts in the middle ages, which, unfortunately, seems to have been lost. However, if you have only a small amount to store, preserving them in salt is quite a good way. Pick as dry as possible and de-husk and leave on a tray in a warm place, for a few days. Then pack nuts into a jar, using plenty of coarse salt with them. A ½" (1 cm) layer of salt is left on top; it is best to fit a good lid.

Incidentally, if you are disappointed at the small yield in nuts on your first foray to the hazelwoods, do not be disheartened. The weather of the previous late winter and early spring was probably inimical to the fertilising process. You must console yourself with the hope that things will be better next year.

SALTED HAZEL NUTS

Mildly fry hazel nuts in cooking oil or olive oil and make sure they have soaked up a lot of the liquid. (If it is not intended to keep the nuts for too long, butter goes very well in place of oil.) Salt and lightly spice – curry powder or cayenne are recommended – and roll the nuts on a sheet of paper to coat them evenly. Store when cold in grease proof bags and keep as airtight as possible.

HAZEL NUT BUTTER

5 oz (125 g) kernels **1 lb (500 g) butter**

Use, if possible, the traditional home-made butter. Blanch the hazel nuts with boiling water, and cut and pound, sprinkling with a little water, to produce a smooth paste. Mix paste and butter in a bowl and rub through a sieve to complete the process. Keep in airtight containers. It makes an exceptionally good sandwich spread, far better in our opinion than the better-known peanut butter. It may also go well in soups and sauces.

HAZEL NUT AND RAISIN CAKE

4 oz (100 g) chopped hazel nuts
8 oz (250 g) flour
100 ml milk approx.
1 egg
4 oz (100 g) chopped raisins
4 oz (100 g) sugar
Pinch of salt
1 tspn. baking powder

Beat the egg and mix with sugar and milk. Sift the flour and the salt and baking powder and slowly stir the dry mixture into the wet. Add the nuts and fruit. Put into a well greased baking tin and bake for fifty minutes in a moderately hot oven at 400°F (200°C) Reg. 6.

MEADOWSWEET

Filipendula ulmaria

One of the great scents of summer is the fragrance from these frothy masses of the tiny cream-coloured flowers. The stems, stiff, angular and reddish, will grow up to 4 ft (1¼ m) in height and the irregular, toothed leaflets are dark green above (seen leaning away to the left) but silvery-grey underneath (right).

The most common names for *Filipendula ulmaria* in English and in Irish tell us a great deal about it: Meadowsweet and *Airgead Luachra* ('Rush Silver'). This very common flowering plant grows mostly in damp ground, often in association with rushes, in meadows and near streams; the frothy flowerheads look as if the field had been sprinkled with silver and their very beautiful sweet scent (they are also known as Sweetmeadow, Sweet Hay) gives out one of mid-summer's most characteristic smells. The plant is usually about 2 feet (¾ m) tall but may double that, standing on upright red-green stems. The leaves are of a fine green above and whitish underneath. It flowers from June and is best collected in this month, though it will last until mid-autumn. The flowers are small and cream-white but stand so close together that the cluster looks like one large flower. Care must be taken by the beginner that he or she does not pick dwarf elder instead; the meadowsweet, however, can be readily distinguished by its leaves, green above, silvery below. At any rate, meadowsweet is much the more beautiful of the two as its French name, Queen of the Meadow, and another English one, Maid of the Mead, indicate.

The root was used in fever cures and all drinks made from the flowers were supposed to be very good for skin disorders. Because of their scent, they were also used in sick-rooms and so forth, for scouring vessels and in dye-making. It was also much used in flavouring preserves and wines and, in particular, mead; try the dried leaves, for instance, in your sloe wine to impart a wonderful bouquet. Ideas as regards flavouring may be gleaned from the uses of elderflower in this respect. A good tea may be made from the flowers. It is said that parts of the plant, dried and ground, have been used instead of flour in times of scarcity.

Meadowsweet was a sacred herb in ancient Celtic druidic ritual and this might have led to brides in medieval times wearing garlands woven from the flowers. We love – and agree wholeheartedly with – the opinion of the great Elizabethan herbalist, John Gerard, that it 'makes the heart merrie and delighteth the senses.'

MEADOWSWEET WINE

1 gallon (4½ litres) flowers
½ lb (250 g) chopped raisins
Juice of 1 lemon
2½ lb (1¼ kg) sugar
1 tbspn. cold tea
1 gallon (4½ litres) water
1 tspn. yeast

Pour the boiling water over the flowers, chopped raisins and sugar. Leave for three days, squeezing frequently before straining and adding the yeast, tea, lemon juice and a nutrient, if handy. Ferment to a finish, using extra sugar if necessary and syphoning when required. Some authorities recommend fermenting on the pulp (i.e. all ingredients) for a week or more before transferring to the fermentation jar but, personally, we do not care to try this as there would be a danger of decomposition of vegetable matter if the initial fermentation is not fast enough.

MUSHROOM

Agaricus campestris

Full-grown Field Mushroom is from 1 to 3 inches (2½ - 7½ cm) across its white, smooth cap. The gills are pink when young but gradually darken to a chocolate brown. The stem is normally no shorter nor slimmer than that illustrated overleaf. It will have a ring or traces of one below the cap and this is actually joined to the cap in the immature 'button-top'.

There are several thousand species of fungi growing in these islands of which many are inedible and a very small number are poisonous. Four are fatal to humans – so be warned: make sure it is the real thing when you intend to pick the common Field Mushroom. Not that this fungus is very difficult to recognise: after all, it is mainly children who collect them each year and cases of poisoning are, to our knowledge at any rate, very uncommon.

The Field Mushroom (*Beacán* in Irish Gaelic) is, as one expects from the name, most common in pastures, especially so in those in which horses have been kept. Of course they occur elsewhere, in meadows and in tilled fields, for instance. We recall that once, while out on a stroll, having come on a turnip-field whose drills were speckled white with mushrooms, we filled two opened umbrellas with the spoils and left as much behind us. Presumably, as the tractor has progressively replaced the horse and artificial fertilisers the animal manures, the yield of mushrooms grows less, but once, in the autumn of 1976, we collected two four-stone bags full from a five-acre field and left at least as many behind us.

If in doubt, you should first study cultivated mushrooms, not so much the immature 'button tops' which the public, in its ignorance, insists on buying, but the full-grown fungus. These are very similar to the wild variety. The cap of the field mushroom has pink gills when young, and these gradually turn to a colour that seems chocolate at first sight, but has much of a dark purple in it. The cap itself is white, smooth and milky (this is important) to touch, and, at most, three inches (7½ cm) across (although the horse mushroom, which is also edible and which is very similar otherwise, may grow up to 1 foot (30 cm) across when mature). It should look, smell – and taste – pleasant and wholesome. A good rule is never to eat mushrooms which have white gills under-

neath the cap. Remember too, that you will generally have to scrutinise the ground carefully for mushrooms as they will more often than not be hidden in the grass. Where there is one, there are likely to be others very close by. Don't pluck the mushroom out roughly but twist it gently and it will come away easily, without damage to the root system.

One of the choicest ways of all to cook mushrooms is also the simplest. Bring them straight home, put them cap downwards on top of a hot range or griddle or even a pan will do. (Actually, the best way is on the hot coals of the hearth.) Put a bit of butter to melt in the cap, add salt to taste and eat before it burns.

The wild Field Mushroom can be used in any of the recipes which usually stipulate cultivated mushrooms and the basic method of cooking them is only one step away from the primitive method we used as children. Either fry or grill them with butter, salt and pepper in their caps, or wrap them in kitchen foil and cook in a fairly hot oven for fifteen minutes. It is a good idea to blanch mushrooms in boiling water before submitting them to the harsh heat of the grill.

Mushrooms are easily dried. Remove the stems and thread the well-opened caps on a string with a good knot between each one so as to keep them separated. Hang them in a warm, dry place – near the kitchen work-counter, as on the Continent – but where the steam cannot get at them. When fully dry, they may be kept in jars. They need to be soaked in water until soft if you require them for frying, etc.

A friend of ours from Cavan has told us how the farmers' wives there used to make a simple relish with mushrooms and salt. The mushrooms, as they were collected from day to day, were put in layers into earthenware jars and each layer covered with a layer of salt. As more mushrooms were casually collected, they were added with further layers of salt. The jars were left in a cool place, usually in the dairy, until a thick black relish collected. This was then poured off into bottles. Pepper and onion might be added at this stage.

NETTLE

Urtica dioica

The common, stinging nettle grows coarse and upright to 4 ft (1¼ m) high, flowering from June onwards, but it is not at all advisable to harvest them in their mature state. The tops of young, spring nettles (as shown opposite) are best for eating – and won't trouble you overmuch with stings.

A whimsical tale from ancient times gives us what must be one of the oldest of recipes – and nettles was one of the ingredients. St. Columcille, mortifying himself (and, doubtless, his brethren also) during Lent with only a broth of water, nettles and salt for sustenance, was asked by his distraught cook if nothing else was to go into the cauldron. 'Nothing else will go into the broth', said that stern man with grim humour, 'except what comes out of the pot stick'. With that typical logic which has remained – for better or for worse – an Irish characteristic, the cook hollowed out his pot stick and poured down milk and oatmeal into the broth. The saint, having laid down the rules, had himself to abide by them!

This broth – *Brotchán Neanntóg* – was one of the favourite foods of the Irish people, it would seem, from at least the Early Christian era until the cabbage became common, less than two hundred years ago. Indeed, many of the poorer people relied to a considerable extent on *Brotchán Neanntóg* in this century. Very probably that's what the old woman, mentioned in the famous Fenian ballad, was going to make:

Down by the glenside I met an old woman;
A-plucking young nettles, she ne'er saw me comin',
I listened a while to the song she was hummin' –
'Glory-o, glory-o to the Bould Fenian Men.'

There are, we believe, three native species of nettle, but it is the common stinging nettle with which we are concerned. It never fails to amaze us when people express surprise and even revulsion at the idea of eating what is probably the most common of edible wild plants in this part of the world.

The nettle grows just about everywhere, town and country, where earth has been disturbed. Indeed, it is sometimes possible to divine the existence of old habitation sites from its presence. Here is one herb, surely, which everyone recognises – for who has not been stung by one? As one old herbalist noted wryly, 'the stinging-weed may in emergency be found on the darkest night as well as in daylight'. The poison – formic acid – is, of course, destroyed in the cooking. While it is true that if you grasp a nettle (as the rhyme says) 'like a lad of mettle' it can't sting you, it makes things much easier if you wear gloves while plucking the young plants or shoots for cooking.

There is a folk-saying in Ireland, *Gach n-aon mar a h-oiltear é 's an traona ris an neannta*, 'each one as he is bred and the corncrake loves the nettle'. The corncrake shows good sense for, in the past, the herb has provided an important source of food, animal as well as human, in western Europe and was always considered to be one of the more useful of the wild plants. Believe it or not, a very strong cloth, especially for sheets and tablecloths, was made from it and also fishermen's anchor ropes – and within living memory, at that. World War Two opened the eyes of the enterprising British Ministry of Supply to some of the nettle's possibilities, which included the manufacture of chlorophyll and of a dye used in camouflage work. When we were young, it was thought to make excellent food for turkeys and, though most quadrupeds – the ass is an exception – will refuse it in its natural state, farmers liked to include some quantity of it in hay. Two centuries ago, the Swedes used to cultivate the nettle, using the leaves as food for milch cows and the stalks for the cloth or 'nettle linen'. By the way, both beer and wine have been made from the leaves in the past. (As we write this a gallon of nettle wine is gaily fermenting above our heads.)

The English seem to have once eaten it as much as the Irish. In 1661, Samuel Pepys recorded in his diary that he enjoyed a bowl of nettle porridge; a century later, the herbalist Brook had this to say about the plant: 'The young shoots or tops are gathered early in the Spring to boil in broth or gruel. The young leaves, eaten in the Spring, are not a bad substitute for spinach'. It is recorded that it was grown under glass in Scotland as 'early kale'; the wild variety was equally popular there in broths and porridge and, of course, in haggis.

The Irish also used it in haggis, which was called *proinnseach* (we give a recipe for a modern version on page 135), in gruels and porridge, as a vegetable and as garnishing. It would seem to have been used in conjunction with (and, as the year wore on, supplanted by) charlock or *praiseach* in porridge. Like the Scots, we looked upon it as 'wild cabbage' or 'wild kale' but, in common with several other plants, it was more commonly known as 'greens' or *glasraí-fáis*.

Nowadays, the very Irish dish, Colcannon, (*cál ceannfhionn*, creamed or buttered kale) is made with cabbage, but doubtless the 'greens' mentioned in the old song about it often included nettles:

Did ye ever ate colcannon that's
made from thickened cream,
With greens and scallions blended
like a picture in your dream?
Did ye ever take a forkful
and dip it in the lake
Of the clover-flavoured butter
which your mother used to make?

It is rarely used in Ireland today except as a medicine for purifying the blood in the spring: some people make an infusion and take a little 'nine days in a row and fasting' while others eat it, boiled like spinach or cabbage, three times before the end of May. Many farmers' wives of the older generation in the Golden Vale diligently served it to their households once a fortnight throughout the spring for its medicinal value. For all we know some still do, though few country people these days will easily admit to ever having used it. This has nothing to do with superstition, as might at first be supposed, but is because nettles, along with most other wild foods, have been associated with poverty and backwardness. The inferiority complex of a people, emerging from some two centuries of famine and severe depressions, runs deep. The *Brotchán* is making something of a comeback, however, and some of the more discerning of hotels have this delicious broth on their menu.

Nettles should not be picked for the pot after the end of May, as by then they have turned coarse and laxative. In March, the small shoots may be picked entire and used; later, just choose the tops and newest leaves. In Irish Gaelic, the young shoots and the cooked vegetable are known as *neanntóga*; the coarse mature plant as *neannta loiscneach* ('burning nettle').

When preparing as a vegetable, remove the tougher stems and wash well. They make a good addition to leeks or cabbage. A common country practice was to have them as a variant of that old favourite, bacon and cabbage; the nettles are cooked in the water in which the bacon has been boiled but it is important to have first removed the meat or it will be dyed an unpleasant colour. They may be used with or in place of the more usual vegetables in the traditional dishes, colcannon, *staimpí* ('champ', 'chop') and Dublin coddle.

When used by themselves, cook as for spinach. In Scotland and in the north of Ireland, boiled chicken has traditionally been cooked with about a half pint (¼ litre) of very finely chopped nettle together with the other ingredients of nettle broth, i.e. oatmeal, butter, leeks, onions or wild garlic. You may also use well-chopped nettles in a modern version of a *proinnseach* (the Scots haggis is the most famous member of this family of puddings). The Scots dish normally includes various parts from the inside of a sheep, minced fine and mixed with suet, but a ½ lb (250 g) of thickly sliced bacon cut into large chunks fits the bill very nicely for others. Mix the bacon and nettles with the chopped leeks and cabbage and about 3 oz (75 g) oatmeal. As you probably will have no sheep's stomach at your hand, put the lot into a muslin bag and boil for an hour or so. Serve with gravy made from the stock or, better still, a white sauce; a knob of butter (especially country butter) on each helping will not go astray if the dish is not already very greasy.

BROTCHÁN NEANNTÓG (NETTLE SOUP) *Serves 6-8*

3¾ pints (1¾ litres) young nettles
3 oz (75 g) porridge oats
2 oz (50 g) butter
¼ pint (150 ml) cream
3 pints (1½ litres) beef or mutton stock
1 egg yolk
2 onions – traditionally leeks were used instead of onions
Salt and pepper

This makes an excellent, well-flavoured, thick soup, much beloved in our house, especially during those very cold spring days which gave rise to the saying, *ní fuacht go hEarrach*, which means something like 'no cold like that of the Spring'. We are inclined to believe that prashock was often used with or instead of the nettles, especially in summertime. We strongly recommend grated nutmeg as additional flavouring; indeed, this soup welcomes your experimenting with traditional herbal seasonings.

Fry the onions in the butter, add the stock, the nettles, finely chopped, the oats and the seasonings. Cook slowly for one hour. Allow the soup to cool somewhat and slowly stir in the beaten egg and cream. Reheat but do not allow to boil. You can use if you wish a selection of spring herbs with the nettle, e.g. dandelion leaves, sorrel, fat hen, etc.

NETTLE GRUEL *Serves 3*

½ pint (¼ litre) chopped nettles
1 oz (25 g) oatmeal
1 oz (25 g) butter
1 pint (½ litre) milk or stock

This was the early spring variant of the traditional *praiseach*, the wholesome pottage so commonly eaten by the poorer classes in Ireland up to a hundred years ago (see under Prashock / Charlock).

Fry the oatmeal in the butter until browned. Then add the stock or milk, whichever you have chosen, and bring to the boil. Add the finely chopped nettles and cook slowly for a few minutes. Season with salt as required while cooking. Alternatively, boil the nettles in the liquid and cook until tender. Drain (retaining the stock) and chop finely, press through a sieve if desired. Return purée to the stock adding the oatmeal with seasoning to taste. Simmer and stir for a few minutes. Mix in some butter or cream or even a little bacon fat and serve hot.

NETTLE BEER

1 gallon (4½ litres) nettles
1 gallon (4½ litres) water
1 lb (500 g) sugar
yeast
½ oz (10 g) root ginger (optional)
1 oz (25 g) hops (optional)
1 oz (25 g) cream of tartar
1 lemon

Use only young nettles and rinse them well. Continue as for Dandelion Beer (page 94). The hops, if used, go in along with the nettle tops; you may also prefer to use more than one lemon, when you come to make this a second time.

NETTLE WINE

2 qts (2 litres) young nettle tops
3 lb (1½ kg) sugar
2 lemons
½ oz (10 g) ginger
1 gallon (4½ litres) water
yeast

Rinse the nettle tops before simmering in enough water to cover, with the ginger and peel (without pith) of one lemon for about forty-five minutes. After straining, add enough water to bring the amount of must up to a gallon (4½ litres). Add the sugar, the lemon juice and nutrient, stir to dissolve, and add the yeast when cool. Keep fermenting quickly in a covered container for four days and then ferment in the fermentation jar at the usual speed. Syphon as the wine begins to clear and leave for some three months before racking and bottling.

PLUM

Prunus domestica, etc.

Though generally bigger (growing up to 20 ft (6 m) and more in height) than their cousin, the blackthorn, wild plums often bear a distinct resemblance to the latter. The slightly toothed, elliptical leaves are broader, however, and the 'spines' do not develop but remain as short, if somewhat jagged shoots as at bottom left. The pendulous, round, crab apple sized fruits (with their typical plum stones) come in various guises, some trees bearing sloe-coloured 'damsons' (opposite) while others have yellow-greenish fruit.

Tá biolar in san abhainn ann agus gall-chnóa ar chrann ann,
Duille breá glas agus sméartha,
Seilíní a's áirní, ubhla a's baláistí,
Agus meas ag fás ar bharr géag ann.

'There's cress in the river there and walnuts on the trees there, fine fresh leaves and berries, cherries and sloes, crab apples and bullaces and mast growing on the tips of the branches.'
Raifterí (1784-1835)

Wild plums are a lot more common than most people think. The Sloe, fruit of the Blackthorn, is itself a variety of the plum family *Rosaceae*, but because of its distinctive qualities is treated in this book under the heading 'Blackthorn.' Here we are concerned with several other members of the plum family, the native wild plums and the garden varieties gone wild and those which are a cross between the two. Indeed, it is next to impossible for the amateur to distinguish between the different varieties; very often we find that country people refer to the 'black' plums as damsons or mazzers and to the 'white' ones as plums, bullaces or creggs.

The common bullace is native to these islands, but probably a great deal of the wild plums are garden plums gone wild. Wild plums and cherries of various kinds are quite common in Co. Limerick and this is an area which was once noted for the number of its orchards. In England, too, it would seem that wild plums are much more likely to be found near the ruined site of an orchard. Add to that the fact that the most common words in Irish Gaelic for these fruits

would seem to be *plumaí* and *baláistí*, both words being obvious corruptions of 'plums' and 'bullaces', and it would seem that the native plum (outside of the sloe) was never very common. By the way, 'bullace' itself is of French origin, as also is 'damson' which means 'plum of Damascus'. We are unable to throw any light on the origin of the 'cregg'. But we cannot eat the roots of words and the most important thing about all wild plums is that they are not only edible but usually delicious when cooked. In fact, they may be treated in the same way as are the domesticated varieties; but it is wise to taste them before cooking and add extra sugar if you feel it is required. They are excellent for jams and tarts.

Normally, the plum trees are medium-sized, up to 20 feet (6 m) high, oftentimes resembling the blackthorn though not by any means as knotty or snaggy, although they may sometimes have thorns. The fruit varies a great deal but is generally somewhat smaller than crab apples, roundish, yellow-green (thus those are often called 'greengages', of course) or white or black-purple; they contain a stone. Some varieties may ripen in September but generally the bullace is at its best in October and even early November. By the way, the old folk would not pick the darker plums until after the first good frost. Remember also that the 'bloom', the dusty, powdery colouring on the skins of plums (very noticeable on the black varieties), is yeast.

PLUM JAM

Jams from all the wild plums, known variously as bullaces, damsons, plums, creggs, etc., may be made in the same way as given below. The recipe includes apples but, if you wish to use the plums by themselves, the same recipe will apply, the general rule being that the weight of the fruit should at least be equalled by the weight of the sugar: as wild plums vary so much with regard to sweetness, always test before boiling. Plums are rich in pectin and therefore do not require the addition of apples, but we have found the following mixture excellent.

3 lb (1½ kg) white bullaces
2 lb (1 kg) apples or crab apples
5 lb (2½ kg) sugar
Juice of ½ lemon

Peel, core and slice the apples. Cook the fruits until soft in approximately a half pint (quarter litre) of water. Combine the sugar, lemon juice and the pulp, and when the sugar is dissolved, boil rapidly, stirring constantly. As they rise to the surface, remove the stones with a draining spoon and put them in a bowl with hot water so as to clean the jam off them, this water being later added to the jam. Test for a set and proceed as advised in the section on jam making.

PLUM AND ELDERBERRY JAM

2 lb (1 kg) plums
2 lb (1 kg) elderberries
4 lb (2 kg) sugar
½ pint (¼ litre) water

Bring the elderberries to the boil in a quarter-pint (150 ml) of water and simmer for a few minutes, then strain overnight. Simmer the plums in a quarter-pint (150 ml) water until tender. Stir in the elderberry juice and then warmed sugar. When the sugar is dissolved, boil rapidly until setting point is reached and proceed as usual. During both simmering and boiling, the stones will have been rising to the surface where they may be removed with a straining spoon; the stones are then put into a bowl with hot water so as to clean off the jam and this is added to the rest before a 'set' is reached. (As wild plums vary greatly in sweetness – or lack of it! – don't forget to test when adding sugar.)

PLUM BUTTER

4 lb (2 kg) sweet wild plums
3 lb (1½ kg) sugar

Barely cover fruit in water and cook until tender. Rub through a fine sieve. Add sugar to pulp and stir until dissolved. Boil rapidly, stirring continuously until the following test tells you the 'butter' is ready: a spoonful of the 'butter', allowed to pour back into the pan, does so in a thin 'sheet' from the lip of the spoon. (Do not boil so long as to cause the preserve to lump in the pan or become so thick as to adhere to the spoon.)

PLUM PIE

Make a base of your favourite short crust pastry; ours is described under Blackberry Pie (page 64). Stone the plums and stew gently in a little water, adding sugar to taste. Strain off and reserve the juice. Place the cooked fruit onto the cooked pastry base. Thicken the plum juice with cornflour, approx. 1 oz (25 g) cornflour to a half pint (quarter litre) juice, and pour over the fruit. Serve hot or cold with cream.

PLUM WINE

Wild plums, bullaces, damsons, even cherries may be treated in the same way. However, as they vary a great deal in sweetness, it is best to taste them first to see how bitter they may be; 4 lb (2 kg) of very sweet bullaces will require only 2 lb (1 kg) sugar while bitter plums will take extra. We would prefer to use raisins with any kind of plum wine, as they are noted for their failure to possess 'body'; many winemakers add a handful of wheat or barley to counteract this. Indeed, they would probably recommend a 1 lb (500 g) or two more of plums than we have given below, while eschewing the raisins altogether. And they would be quite right! For, while agreeing that good wine may be made from plums, we have never made anything other than a very small quantity, preferring to keep the fruit for jam, there being so many other more abundant bases for wine.

4 lb (2 kg) plums
2 – 3 lb (1½ kg) sugar
1 gallon (4½ litres) water
½ lb (250 g) raisins
Pectin-destroying enzyme
1 tspn. yeast

If you feel that the wild yeasts are unreliable, wipe the plums first of all. Prick the skins with a fork and pour the boiling water over them; if you mash them (don't break the stones) or even cut them up, it is as well when straining to use two thicknesses of muslin. Include the chopped raisins and sugar with the plums, cover well and leave for four days, having added the enzyme when cool. Stir or bruise daily. After straining, add the yeast and ferment quickly for a week or two. Transfer to the fermentation jar (the liquor may need skimming first of all), syphon when clear and bottle when fermentation is absolutely finished. Be extra careful as regards completion of fermentation, which may take anything up to six months. Rack, bottle and mature for at least three months.

PRASHOCK / CHARLOCK

Sinapsis arvensis

A very variable plant with many different forms, whose erect, well-branched stem may grow to well over 12 inches (30 cm) in height. However, especially when young, it may appear like the plant at right (overleaf) and may even remind one of a young cabbage plant. The leaves, sometimes notched, tend to bear some resemblance to those of its relatives, turnip, parsnip and the older forms of cabbage. The flower has four bright yellow petals (with four spreading sepals) and the plant may look very pretty indeed but, as it grows taller (left-hand illustration), it tends to become coarse and rank.

The story is told of a poor man who went courting a widow's daughter and who was given a reluctant welcome by the mother. The girl's prospects not being of the very best, however, the widow was preparing a pot of gruel or 'stirabout' made with prashock for the visitor when another suitor, the son of a 'stronger' farmer, arrived on the scene. Better fare was promptly produced, whereupon the poor man said grace as follows:

Oh God be praised, I am amazed
to see how things have ended:
Spuds and butter for the tay
when shtirabout was intended!

Not even the nettle has had such abuse heaped on it as has charlock or prashock (as it is more commonly termed in Ireland, being a slight corruption of the Gaelic *praiseach*). As early as the seventeenth century, the term of abuse, *giolla na praisce* (which might be loosely translated as 'charlock-eater' or 'porridge-eater') was in use; the eighteenth century Ulster poet, Séamus Dall Mac Cuarta, in verses describing the Contention of the Seasons, makes winter boast: *Cha bhím-sa mar an Earrach ag ithe neanntóg ná praisigh*, 'I'm not like the Spring eating nettles or charlock-porridge.' Several folk-sayings, none of them complimentary, were based on the image of charlock gruel or porridge. *Tá an praiseach ar fud na mias agat*, they'd say – 'you've made a mess of things' or, literally, 'you've (got) the gruel all over the (milk) basins.' Another is a reminder of the days when people were obliged to sit around the one pot and eat from it: *Tá tusa chomh doimhin sa phraiseach le h-aoinne acu,* 'You're involved in the trouble as much as anyone' or, literally, 'You're as deep in the porridge as any of them'. Indeed, the common word in Irish Gaelic for a 'mess' is *praiseach* and, to this day in many parts of the country, if someone feels that you are talking nonsense or 'hot air', they will dismiss you with the one word, 'Prashock!' And it is not only in Ireland that charlock is denigrated. Some years ago, an English botanist described it in print as a 'vegetable rat' (because it is so difficult to eradicate it from wherever it has seeded).

Yet the lowly charlock has saved entire communities during periods of famine and hardship in Britain (especially in the western islands) and in Ireland, even up to the last century. Not only that, but in this country, at least, it has constituted a staple food for the poorer people at certain times of the year. Consider that about a century and a half ago, just prior to the Great Famine, the third month of summer was known as *July an chabáiste,* i.e. 'July of the cabbage', the reason being that, while waiting for the potato crop to mature, the poorer peasants relied on the cabbage for survival. Now, although the Celts cultivated this latter vegetable in Gaul, it would appear that cabbage as we know it was not commonly grown in the field here until the late eighteenth century. The question then arises: what greens did the poor rely on before the advent of cabbage? It is true that a wide assortment of 'greens' were in use from early times, among them wild cabbage and kale, spinach and mustard, but as these were neither plentiful nor possessed the great leaves of the cultivated varieties of greens, they were mostly used for flavouring and garnishing. Besides the watercress, then, the people relied to a great extent on the abundant nettle (in spring) and on prashock, as the year wore on.

In fact, so great was the dependence on prashock that we are not surprised to learn that it was sold in the Dublin markets as a spinach in the eighteenth century, before cabbage came on the scene. It is mentioned in a medieval tale and there is reliable evidence that, during World War Two, a porridge made from it and linseed was eaten in Co. Cavan. So common was prashock in porridge and gruel that *praiseach* became the name for the Indian or Yellow Meal porridges introduced in the nineteenth century. As it was used both in conjunction with and as a substitute for nettles, prashock may be used in most of the nettle recipes given in this book, in the broth and haggis and colcannon for instance. As far as possible, use prashock with a meat stock for a base (*praiseach feola*); for example, if you have boiled a chicken, cut up prashock leaves very finely and cook them in the boiling broth. When preparing as a vegetable, cook in the basic manner as for all wild greens, putting it in a very little salted

water or stock, with a good knob of butter. And, of course, don't forget that that most-maligned dish with such an honourable record, Prashock Stirabout, is made the same way as Nettle Gruel (page 135).

Bíonn blas milis ar phraiseach na gcomharsan, they used to say: 'There's a sweet taste to a neighbour's prashock-gruel' – a typically ironic reference to the hard times, which indicates that prashock may be as bitter as you would expect the first cousin of wild mustard (*praiseach garbh*) to be. We have eaten prashock which has been as sweet as the sweetest green cabbage and have tasted other (from the stalk) which seemed so sour as to make us wonder if prashock would suit the modern taste at all. Tastes *do* change: just think that in former times potatoes and greens were often dressed with sour cream *and* with leeks and onions to boot. We found that the plant with the leaves most resembling those of young cabbage or kale was genuinely tasty – and bore out the opinion of the County Limerick man who told us how he'd 'always save it when weeding the potato field for no cabbage was as sweet.'

We are inclined to think that 'prashock' (or 'preeshaugh') was applied by most people to several members of the *Cruciferae* or Mustard family, including the genus *Brassica*. Some of these are sweeter than others. We repeat that the best plan is to pick those leaves which most resemble cabbage or kale (which are, incidentally, two other members of the Mustard family). The leaves should be gathered when young – indeed, they look most like small cabbage leaves then. Sweet or sour, however, they are an excellent source of vitamins A, B and C. In addition, they supply necessary bulk and fibre so lacking in our modern diet.

ROSE

Rosa canina

An erect but straggly shrub, 3 - 10 ft (1–3 m) high, which often, with the aid of its cruel thorns, uses a neighbouring bush for support. The sharply toothed leaves have five to seven somewhat downy leaflets. The simple five-petalled, white-pink rose of mid summer gives way to the characteristic orange-red, oblong berries, something shorter than 1 inch (2½ cm) in length.

'Tis there's a strand too, that's decked with car-weeds
And tender gob-stones and mussel-shells;
And there's skeehories and what still more is
A comely fresh-flowering water-rill.
– late eighteenth century comic song.

There are several kinds of wild roses, but the Dog Rose (*Rosa Canina*) is by far the most common, growing mainly in hedgerows and rough ground and often in amongst brambles; although more plentiful in the southern parts of these islands, it is usually so abundant that you rarely need to travel too far to collect a reasonable amount of berries. They have many local names. Amongst those common in Ireland are Magories and Johnny McRorys (which are corruptions of the Gaelic *Mugóire*, itself a corruption of *Mucóir*, meaning the fruit of the *Sceachóir Muc* or Pig Rose); Itchy-backs (because of its tendency to cause itching if – a trick beloved of schoolboys – squeezed down the back of someone's neck); Buckle Berries (a term confined to the northern end of the country). Names for the Dog Rose common all over Britain and Ireland are Briar and Hip-tree; the Sweetbriar (Irish Gaelic, *Sceach Chumhra* or 'fragrant thorn-bush') is a different variety. We have always been intrigued as to how the Dog Rose got its name; it has a similar name in Irish Gaelic, *Coindris* (or 'Hound Thorn') and the hip itself is *Sceachóir Madraigh* (or 'Dog's Thorn-berry'); most often, it is simply called *Sceachóid*, indicating the fruit of a thorny tree, or *Sceachóir*, whence comes another common name, Skeehories. The flower, of course, is *Rós* (in Scotland, *Ros*) and there are several Gaelic words, formed on the base *dris* ('thorn'), which do the work of the English 'briar'. The Welsh is *Rhosyn gweyllt* ('wild rose').

June is the month of the flower, though it may bloom as early as late April. The five-petalled flowers are white or pale pink. In July, these begin to shed their petals and this is the time to pick them – that is, when the petals will come away with the gentlest pull. They were usually used in salads and for winemaking, but here on the coast of western Europe we have never put the flower of the wild rose to the more exotic uses they have for it in the Middle East and also in eastern Europe. However, in Ireland at least, the roots were used in the treatment of wool and in dyeing and for making the cores of hurling balls and handballs. Of course, they have provided pipe bowls for centuries and the berries have been used for dye, flavouring and jellies. The petals have also been medically used.

The eye-catching orange-red fruit appears in late August; however, if you wish to use them straight away, do not pick until frost has softened them somewhat, say, in early October. Although many may remain on the trees throughout the winter, they will be of little use after October has gone – remember the old folk belief that the *Púca* breathes on all wild fruits at Hallowe'en. The best berries will be found higher up the bush, which will be anything from 4 to 10 ft (1–4 m) high, so come prepared as the thorn of the wild rose is not famed in proverbs and ballads for nothing.

It is very important that all should know that the seeds of the hips are covered with potentially dangerous hairs, especially damaging to children. If jam is being made, then the seeds must be removed from the flesh of the hip and, in making jellies or syrup, a very fine jelly bag is used (page 42).

ROSEHIP SYRUP *(1)*

2 lb (1 kg) rosehips
1 lb (500 g) sugar
3 pints (1½ litres) water

Treat the hips as described above. Mince, grate or crush the flesh of the fruit and put straight away into the boiling water. Bring back to boiling point before removing from the heat. Stand for a quarter of an hour and then strain carefully through a very fine jelly bag. Return the pulp to the pan, add a further 1½ pints (¾ litre) boiling water and proceed as before. Boil all the juice together until reduced to 1½ pints (¾ litre) (don't forget to have thoroughly cleaned your pan of all pulp, etc.). Add 1 lb (500 g) warmed sugar, stir to dissolve and boil for a further five minutes. While still hot, pour into warmed bottles and seal immediately. Sterilize as advised in the section on making syrups.

ROSEHIP SYRUP *(2)*

This method we have not used but we give it as it is an example of an older way of making syrup. The hips were gathered before the first frosts. It is absolutely necessary to cut the hips open and to remove all the seed and pith; only the flesh is used. Leave in a non-metal dish (with occasional stirring) until soft enough to be put through a sieve. An equal amount in weight of sugar is stirred into the purée. Add ¼–½ pint (150–300 ml) water per lb (500 g) of original weight of hips. Bring slowly to the boil. Skim, bottle while hot and sterilize. To make a nice dessert, mix a few tablespoons cornflour to a paste in water, mix into the syrup and bring to the boil, stirring well. Serve hot or cold with cream.

ROSEHIP PURÉE

Desserts, especially filling for tarts, were commonly made from this purée in medieval times. The hips were gathered before the first frosts. It is absolutely necessary to cut them open and to remove all the seed and pith; only the flesh is used. They are left in a non-metal dish (a Kilner jar or old-fashioned earthenware jar will do fine), with occasional stirring, until soft enough to put through a sieve. An equal weight of sugar is mixed through the purée, the whole being warmed and stirred to dissolve the sugar. Bottle and sterilize. See also under Rosehip Syrup (2) for dessert.

ROSEHIP AND CRAB APPLE JAM

Equal amounts of hips and crabs may be used. Treat the hips as described on page 42. Slice the crabs and cook to a pulp. Stir in the rosehip juice and then add the warmed sugar at the rate of 1 lb (500 g) per lb (500 g) of crabs. Stir until the sugar dissolves, testing for sweetness. Boil quickly until jam sets when tested. Skim and proceed as advised in the section on jam making.

ROSEHIP AND CRAB APPLE JELLY

See under Crab Apple and Rosehip Jelly (page 85).

ROSEHIP TEA

Take about a cupful of hips, cut them or crush them with a mallet or (better still) grind them on a coarse mincer and put them immediately into about ½ gallon (2 litres) of boiling water. They may be simmered for half an hour before straining, but we prefer to leach them overnight before so doing. Straining well is of the utmost importance. Two thicknesses of butter muslin, a flannel or linen crash jelly bag will do for a strainer. Allow to drip until the greater amount of the liquid has come through, but do *not* squeeze. (If required, you may now return the pulp to the saucepan, add about a ½ pint (¼ litre) of boiling water and run through the jelly bag twice). Quickly bring tea to the boil and bottle into hot sterile jars with a good sealing top – Kilner jars are excellent for this. Sweeten with sugar or honey when reheated. (Use small containers as the tea will not keep for more than a week once the jar has been opened.)

ROSEHIP WINE

2 lb (1 kg) hips
1 lemon
1 orange
1 gallon (4½ litres) water
3 lb (1½ kg) sugar
1 tspn. pectin-destroying enzyme
yeast
yeast nutrient

Treat the berries as in Rosehip Tea before adding them to the boiling water. When cool, add the juice and rind (without white pith) of the lemon and orange and also the pectin-destroying enzyme. Leave for twenty-four hours and strain carefully (see Rosehip Tea above). Add the sugar and, when dissolved, add the yeast and nutrient and ferment to a finish, racking when necessary. This is a good simple method, but you will probably get better results if you ferment quickly on the pulp for a fortnight before straining. When wine clears (after about three months), syphon or rack; leave for a further three months, before again racking and bottling.

ROSEHIP SYRUP WINE

We would prefer to make wines in the winter months from syrups we have prepared the previous summer and autumn than to use dried fruits. The following method may be used with any of the syrups mentioned in this book.

About 8 oz (250 g) of syrup (enough to fill a small mineral water bottle) is sufficient to make a gallon (4½ litres) of wine. Merely bring the water to the boil, add the syrup, stir well to dissolve and later add the yeast; it is wise to always add yeast nutrient and a pectin-destroying enzyme. Pour into the fermentation jar and ferment quickly in a warm place. After a week, top up to the bottom of the neck with cold boiled water and ferment to a finish in a cooler place. It may be necessary to keep adding sugar to keep fermentation going as long as possible.

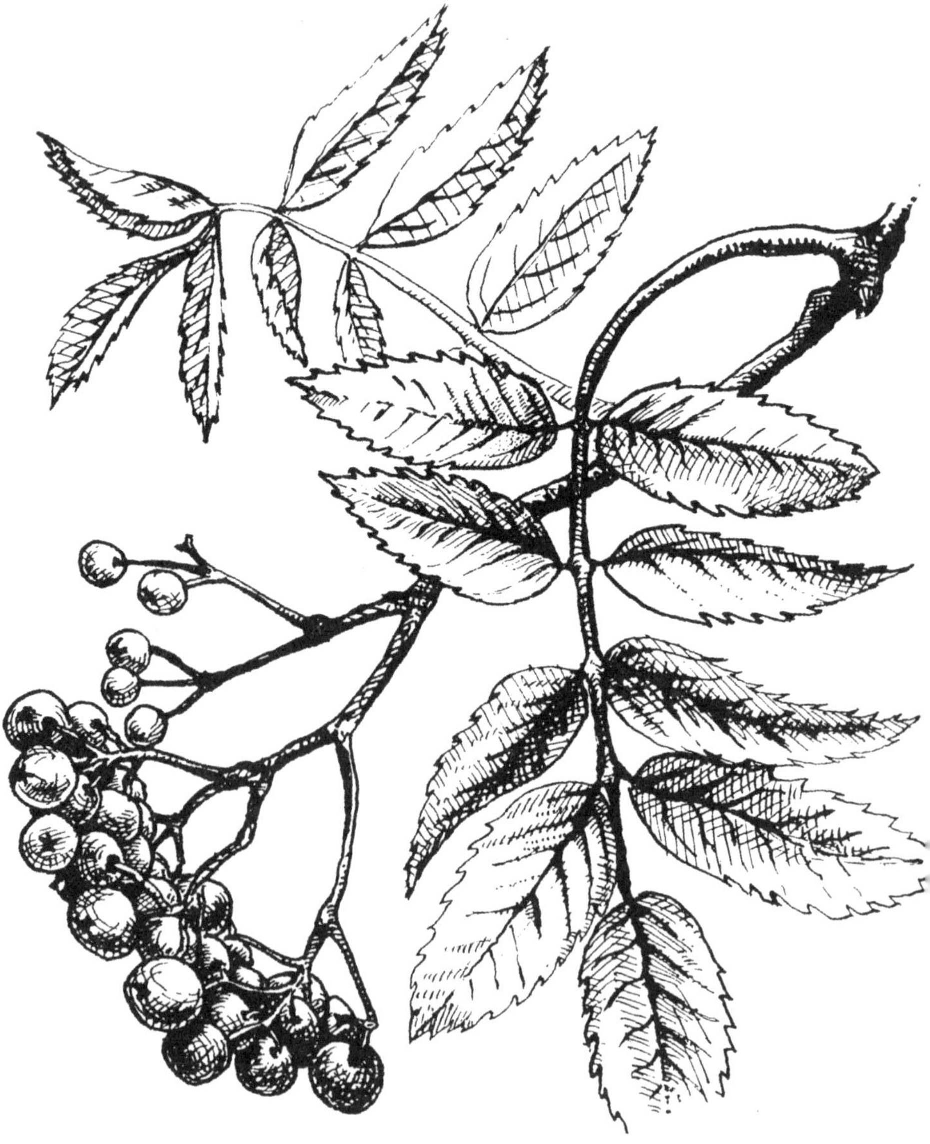

ROWANTREE

Sorbus aucuparia

This graceful, ornamental tree (so suitable for suburban street planting) is usually a lot smaller than its potential 40 ft (12 m). It has lovely, warm-grey bark, smooth and skin-like with occasional wrinkles. The graceful leaves have 9–15 leaflets, lance-shaped and sharply toothed, which turn to beautiful yellows and reds. Large clusters of the bright orange berries (pea-sized and pungently sour) blaze on the autumn landscape.

'Creud iad na caora úd iarrus Fionn,' do ráidh Gráinne, 'mar nach bhféidir a bhfagháil dó?' 'Atá,' ar Diarmuid, 'crann caorthainn d'fhágaibh Tuatha Dé Danann a dtriucha céad Ó bhFiachrach; agus gach caor dá dtig ar an gcrann san bíd buadha iomdha aco .i. bíonn meisge fíona agus sásamh sein-mhidh ann gach caor díobh; agus gidh bé chaithfeas trí chaora díobh dá mba slán a cheud bliadhain dó, do rachfadh a n-aois a dheich mbliadhain fithchead.'

'What are these berries which Fionn requires,' asked Gráinne, 'that they cannot be obtained for him?' 'They are', said Diarmuid, 'those of a rowantree the People of the Goddess Dana left in the territory of O Fiachraigh; and every berry that comes on that tree has great virtues, i.e. there is the intoxication of wine and the satisfaction of old mead in each berry of them; and whosoever eats three of those berries, even if he were a hundred years old, his age would return to ten and twenty years.'

– medieval Ossianic tale

The Scots call the tree Rowantree, (probably from a Scandinavian root) and it is known by this name, or that of Roantree, all over Ireland and much of Britain. The name Mountain Ash is also common. In Ireland, too, it has also been called the Quickentree, a name not so widespread now as it would seem to have been once; possibly, this is a corruption of the Irish Gaelic *Caorthann*. The usual name for a red berry in Irish is *caor* and this is especially applied to the Rowan or mountain berry. Scots Gaelic *Caorunn* and Welsh *Cerddin* are closely related names to the Irish.

The tree is most often found on hillsides, but also on rocky land and in hillside woods, and is most common to the north and west of the British Isles.

It is difficult to describe but, once seen blazing with berries on an autumn landscape, it is unforgettable. Incidentally, the rowantree is proving very popular nowadays in parks and by streets. The tree is generally small, delicate-looking and grey barked; it will grow up to 40 feet (12 m) high, but half this is more common. Its distinctive leaflets are uniform, pinnate, even fernlike. Its flowers, which bloom in late April and early May, are small and white, with a light, almond-like scent. By September, the flowers have turned into large clusters of brilliant, orange-red berries, very juicy and very, very bitter. The berries can be expected to be at their best in October; they may hang on the tree in a mild winter until it is virtually the calendar spring, but surely 'go off' after November – remember the folk belief that at Hallowe'en the *púca* breathes on all wild fruits, spoiling them. When gathering the fruit, take the entire cluster (to avoid tedium and waste); the stalk can be trimmed later.

I remember as children we looked upon the tree with a kind of primeval dread and consequently accepted without question that its berries were malignantly poisonous! Obviously, this arose from some kind of debased folk tradition, for the tree has been associated from time immemorial not only with the black arts, but also with warding off evil spirits and witches; indeed, it is recorded that the Druids held it sacred. A far better recommendation, perhaps, is the age-old belief in its rejuvenation properties.

The Celtic peoples certainly fermented the fruit into a wine and the Scots, especially, distilled it to a powerful spirit. The ancient Irish used it to flavour alcoholic drinks, especially their mead (a wine made from honey and barley). The bark was much prized by tanners, its timber considered valuable and its berries were also used in dyeing. In recent times, its most common use has been as a tart but agreeable jelly that is the traditional accompaniment of venison; some relish the jelly with pork and, indeed, most meats. This jelly is a dark orange with a marmalade-like flavour; in our recipes, it is combined with other fruits, apples especially, to help it set better and make it less tart.

ROWANBERRY AND CULTIVATED APPLE JAM

3 lb (1½ kg) rowanberries
3 lb (1½ kg) apples
5½ lb (3 kg) sugar

Peel, core and slice the apples and boil in a little water until soft. Sieve. Cover berries with water and boil for ten minutes, then strain. Combine the juice, the apple pulp and warmed sugar. Boil until the jam sets when tested. Skim and proceed as advised in the section on jam making.

ROWANBERRY AND CULTIVATED APPLE JELLY

If one has a good deal more apples than rowanberries, it may be thought better to use the recipe for Blackberry and Cultivated Apple Jelly (page 67), substituting rowanberries for the blackberries. Otherwise the following proportions should suit.

3 lb (1½ kg) rowanberries
3 lb (1½ kg) apples
2½ pints (1¼ litres) water or cider
Sugar

Cut up the apples and simmer with 2 pints (1 litre) of the water (or cider) until the apples are pulpy. Strain. Now place the rowanberries in the remaining ½ pint (¼ litre) of liquid and simmer slowly until pulpy – not less than 1 hour. Strain. Combine the two juices, measure and to each pint (½ litre) of juice add 1 lb (500 g) sugar. Dissolve over low heat and then boil rapidly until it sets when tested. Skim and proceed in the usual manner.

ROWANBERRY AND BLACKBERRY JELLY

See under Blackberry and Rowanberry Jelly (page 68).

ROWANBERRY AND CRAB APPLE JELLY

See under Crab Apple and Rowanberry Jelly (page 86).

ROWANBERRY WINE

3 lb (1½ kg) rowanberries
3 lb (1½ kg) sugar
1 gallon (4½ litres) water
Juice and rind (without white pith) of 1 lemon
1 lb (500 g) raisins
1 tspn. yeast

This may be made by the same method as that given Blackberry Wine (page 69). Otherwise, pour the boiling water on the berries and leave for four days before straining, squeezing as usual. Add the chopped raisins, lemon and sugar, stirring until sugar is dissolved; then add yeast (and nutrient if you like). Cover well, ferment quickly for a fortnight, strain and ferment to a finish, syphoning, etc. as described in the section on winemaking.

WATERCRESS

Rorippa nasturtium-aquaticum

Two different types of watercress and their hybrid or 'cross' often grow together and on the left is shown the succulent, young spring plant of one variety. The stem grows on a creeping rootstock up to 2 ft (½ m) in length, part of it over or on top of the water. The leaves are dark green and smooth and may remind one of its cousins, the cabbage and prashock; smallish, somewhat spade-shaped, they grow in pairs of one to four. The small, white flowers are evident during summer and early autumn.

Large and profitable are the stacks upon the ground
Uileacan Dubh O!
The butter and the cream do wondrously abound;
Uileacan Dubh O!
The cresses on the water and the sorrels are at hand,
And the cuckoo's calling daily his note of music bland,
And the bold thrush sings so bravely his song i' the
forests grand,
On the fair hills of holy Ireland.
Sir Samuel Ferguson (translated from the Irish)

Probably the best-known of all the wild salads, watercress was a staple food in these islands until modern times. A most valuable and savoury source of Vitamin C, it was being sold in large quantities in the cities up to a century ago. Watercress is perennial and is therefore available during winter and it is quite common, even abundant, where proper conditions are present in ditches and shallow running water.

One must be careful, however, not to pick watercress from stagnant pools and water which flows through sheep pastures as this could be dangerous (the danger here is liver-fluke). It has to be washed very thoroughly before eating, more especially in these pollution-haunted days.

Its pale green stalks are round, quite thick and hollow, with many branches. The young leaves are a fresh, bright green but those of the older plants (which are best for eating) may be a good deal darker. It flowers from mid-summer to mid-autumn, in clusters at the top of the plant. It is sometimes called Tongue Grass or Water Grass in Ireland; in Irish Gaelic, it is *biolar uisce*. The Scots know it as Well-girse while in Yorkshire it is called Tang-tongues.

Watercress may be stewed but perhaps is best eaten raw as a green salad or garnish. Its individual taste goes well when cooked in the pot with boiled bacon, a traditional Irish partnership before the advent of cabbage; use at least a pound (500 g) for a 4 lb (2 kg) ham. Traditionally, it was also used as a garnish with cow-parsnip and was cooked, it would seem, with or in place of nettles in gruels and soups.

WATERCRESS SOUP *(1) Serves 4-6*

3 pints (1½ litres) watercress
3 or 4 leeks or onions
2 pints (1 litre) stock
Butter
Cream
Fennel

This makes a fine soup on a cold day; as the old people used to say, 'There's atin' and drinkin' in it.' Chop the leeks or onions very finely and fry gently in butter to make them tender before adding 1 pint (½ litre) stock and bringing to the boil. Put to one side but keep mixture warm. Do exactly the same with the cress but simmer for ten to fifteen minutes. Mix with the leek soup and add in a little cream (or beaten egg and cream, as in *Brotchán Neanntóg* (page 134). Stir in a few forkfuls of chopped fennel.

WATERCRESS SOUP *(2) Serves 4-6*

2 pints (1 litre) watercress
1 or 2 medium onions
1 large potato
Dessertspoonful of chopped fennel (optional)
¼ pint (150 ml) cream or ½ pint (¼ litre) milk
1½ pints (¾ litre) white stock
1–2 oz (25–50 g) butter

For this much more sophisticated recipe, you must remember to keep a handful of the watercress aside for the garnish. Melt the butter in a saucepan, add the finely-chopped onion and fry gently until soft but not browned. Add the potato, peeled and sliced, and fry gently for five minutes; add the stock and bring to the boil and simmer for fifteen minutes. Now add the chopped watercress and simmer for a further fifteen minutes.

Remove from the heat and either press through a sieve, or better still use an electric blender. Season, return to the stove and bring to the boil before placing to one side and adding the cream or milk. Chop the leafy parts and top parts of the watercress stalks which have been set aside for the garnish and add it and the chopped fennel.

INDEX TO WILD FOOD

INDEX TO RECIPES